P. D. Ouspensky

Psychological Lectures
1934 – 1940

ISBN-13: 978-0-9572481-5-1
ISBN-10: 0-9572481-5-6

bookstudio.co.uk

CONTENTS

FIRST LECTURE

Study of psychology.   Low level of modern psychology.   Origin and meaning of psychology.   Definitions of psychology.   Is psychology a new science?   Fear of psychology.   Disguises of psychology.   Psychology and
philosophy.   Psychology and religion.   Psychology and art.   Psychology
and the evolution of man.   Is the evolution of man possible?   What it
can mean.   Man as he thinks himself to be.   Man as he is.   Man as he
can become.   Conditions of development of man.   What man ascribes to
himself and what he really possesses.   Man does not know himself.   He
can do nothing.   He is not one.   He is not conscious.   He has no permanent 'I'.   He has no will.   Many 'I's in man.   Picture of man.   Danger
of attempts to change oneself without knowledge or method.   Study of
consciousness.   Degrees of consciousness.   Four states of consciousness
possible for man.   Memory and consciousness.   Acquiring control of the
three states of consciousness.

I shall speak about the study of psychology, but I must warn
you that the psychology about which I shall speak is very
different from anything you may know under this name.

To begin with I must say that practically never in history
has psychology stood at *so low a level* as at the present time. It
has lost all touch with its *origin and its meaning*, so that now it
is even difficult to define the term 'psychology', i.e. to say what
psychology is and what it studies. And this is so in spite of the
fact that never in known history have there been so many psychological theories and so many psychological writings.

Later on I shall give several definitions of psychology, but
first we must try to see how psychology can be divided, i.e.
whether there are different kinds of psychology and how they
can be studied.

Psychology is sometimes called a new science. This is quite
wrong. Psychology is, perhaps, the *oldest science* and, unfortunately, in its most essential features, a *forgotten science*.

1

In order to understand how psychology can be divided, it is necessary to realize that psychology, except in modern times, has never existed under its own name. People—and especially those who represented learning in different periods—have always been very suspicious of psychology and afraid of it. And so psychology has had to use different disguises.

For thousands of years it existed under the name of philosophy. Even quite recently, in the last decades of the nineteenth century, many works of psychology were classified as philosophy. And in spite of the fact that almost all the sub-divisions of philosophy, such as logic, the theory of cognition, ethics, aesthetics, referred to the work of the human mind or senses, psychology was regarded as inferior to philosophy and as relating only to the lower or more trivial sides of human nature.

Parallel with its existence under the name of philosophy, psychology existed even longer in the form of religion. I do not mean that religion and psychology were one and the same thing. But almost every known religion developed some kind of psychological theory and—what is very difficult for us to understand now—sometimes even a certain practice, so that the study of religion very often included in itself the study of psychology.

There are many excellent works on psychology in the religious literature of different countries and epochs. For instance, in early Christianity, there was a collection of books called *Philokalia*, now existing in Greek and in Russian. This is a collection of writings by different authors, used in the Eastern Church especially for the instruction of monks. Later I shall refer to the *Philokalia*.

During the time when psychology was connected with philosophy and religion, it also existed in the form of art. Poetry, drama, sculpture, even architecture were means for transmitting psychological knowledge. For instance, the Gothic cathedrals were really treatises on psychology.

Before philosophy, religion and art had taken their separate forms as we now know them, psychology had existed in the form of mysteries, such as those of Egypt and of ancient Greece. Later, after the disappearance of the mysteries, psychology took the form of symbolical teachings, which were sometimes connected with the religion of the period and sometimes not connected, such as astrology, alchemy, magic, and the more modern masonry, occultism and theosophy.

To continue further our analysis of psychological teachings, it is necessary to note that both those which exist openly and those which are hidden can be divided into two chief categories.

First, there are those which study man *as they find him* or *such as they suppose him to be;* and second, those which study man not from the point of view of what he is, but from the point of view of *what he may become,* i.e. from the point of view of his evolution.

When we understand the importance of the study of man from the point of view of his possible development, we shall understand that the first definition of psychology should be that it is the study of man's evolution.

Quite naturally, the most important question in theories of the second kind is whether the evolution of man is a general phenomenon or an exceptional one; i.e. what evolution means in relation to man, what laws govern it, which circumstances and conditions are favourable to it and which are unfavourable.

Here, we shall study only those psychological teachings which refer to the evolution of man; and among them only those which regard the evolution of man as an exceptional phenomenon dependent on certain very rare conditions, both inner and outer.

The fundamental idea in teachings of this kind is that man as we know him is not a completed being, that nature develops him only up to a certain point and then leaves him either to develop further by his own efforts and devices, or to live and die such as he was born.

According to these theories, the evolution of man means the development of certain inner qualities and powers in him which usually remain undeveloped and cannot develop by themselves.

3

Experience and observation show that this development is possible only in certain definite conditions, with efforts of the right kind on the part of man himself, and with sufficient help from those who began similar work before and have already attained a certain degree of development or at least a certain knowledge.

Without efforts, evolution is impossible; without help it is also impossible.

In the way of development, man must become a different being, but all men cannot develop and become different beings. So, in relation to the mass of humanity, evolution is an exception.

These theories of the development of man, taken together, make a certain system which we shall study here.

Many questions naturally arise from the preceding statements.

Which qualities and powers can be developed in man and how can this be done?

What does it mean that man can become a *different being?*

Why can only *a few* men develop and become different beings?

Why all this injustice?

Why cannot *all* men develop and become different beings?

I shall try to answer these questions, and I shall begin with the last: Why cannot all men develop and become different beings?

The answer is very simple.

Because they do not want it.

The fact is that in order to become a different being man must want it *very much* and for a very long time. *The evolution of man depends on his own will.* If man does not want it, or even if he does not want it strongly enough, he will never develop. So there is no injustice. Why should man have what he does not want? If people were forced to become different beings when they are satisfied to be what they are, then *this* would be injustice.

Another very important side of this question is that, in order to 'want' in the right way, man must know not only what he

4

wants but what he may get and how he can get it. Vague desire based chiefly on dissatisfaction with external conditions will not create a sufficient impulse.

Now, the other questions: What does *development* mean and what does *different being* mean?

The answer to these two questions must be divided into two parts.

First, by the way of development man acquires many *new* powers, faculties and properties which now he does not possess and about which he has no idea, or only a very vague and distorted idea.

Second, by the way of development man acquires many powers, faculties and properties *which he also does not possess but which he ascribes to himself, i.e. he thinks he possesses them.*

This is the most important point. By the way of evolution, as described before, i.e. a way based on effort and help, man can acquire qualities which he thinks he already possesses.

In order to understand this better and to know what are these faculties and powers which man can acquire, we must begin with man's general views about himself.

Man does not know himself. He does not realize his own possibilities and his own limitations. He does not even realize to how great an extent he does not know himself.

Man has invented many machines and he knows that any complicated machine needs years of careful study before one can use it or control it. But he does not apply this realization to himself, although he himself is a much more complicated machine than any machine he has invented.

He has all sorts of wrong ideas about himself. First of all he does not realize that he *actually is a machine.*

What does it mean that man is a machine?

It means that he has no *independent movements,* inside or outside of himself. He is a machine which is brought into motion by external influences. All his movements, actions, words, ideas,

5

emotions, moods and thoughts are produced by external influences. By himself he is just an automaton with a certain store of memories of previous experiences and a certain amount of reserve energy.

Man can do nothing. But he does not realize this and ascribes to himself the *capacity to do.*

This must be understood very clearly. *Man cannot do.* Everything that man thinks he does really *happens.* It happens exactly as 'it rains', 'it snows', 'it thaws'.

Unfortunately, in the English language there are no impersonal verbal forms which can be used in relation to human actions. So we must continue to say that man thinks, reads, writes, loves, hates, fights and so on. Actually, all this *happens.*

Man cannot move, think or speak by himself. He is a marionette pulled here and there by invisible strings. If he understands this, he can learn more about himself and possibly even change things for himself. But if he cannot realize and understand his utter mechanicalness, or if he does not wish to accept it as a fact, he can learn nothing more and things cannot change for him.

Man is a machine, but a very peculiar machine. He is a machine which in right circumstances and with right treatment can know itself as a machine, and having fully realized this in general, he may find certain particular movements in himself, which do not happen by themselves but which can be developed only by special work on himself. By developing these movements he can really become a man, i.e. acquire the capacity *to do.* This is a very long process, and very few, even of those who start successfully, come to any tangible results. But if man remains a machine, he can do nothing. Everything happens to him.

Incapacity to do is closely connected with the absence in man of several fundamental features which he also ascribes to himself.

The first is the absence of 'unity', of 'oneness' or 'individuality'.

The second is the absence of permanent ego, or 'I'.

The third is the absence of consciousness.

The fourth is the absence of will.

Man attributes these features to himself in the same way as he attributes to himself the capacity to do. He is convinced that he has individuality, that he has a permanent 'I', that he has will, and that he has consciousness.

All this is an illusion. Man has no unity, no permanent 'I', no consciousness and no will.

He is not *one*, he has not *one* 'I', he consists of hundreds of different 'I's, many of whom do not even know one another.

Every wish, every desire, every 'like' and every 'dislike', every opinion and every tendency, every belief and every disbelief is an 'I'. And each one of them has his own will and his own resistance to the will of other 'I's. These 'I's are divided into groups. Some of these groups are permanent and legitimate, i.e. they correspond to the divisions of man's natural being. Other groups are artificial, invented, imaginary; and they play the most important, and sometimes a most negative, part in human life. We shall come to these groups later.

Now I want to emphasize two facts.

First, I want to repeat what was said before about the absence in man of one permanent controlling 'I' different from other 'I's. All 'I's are equal; it is better to say that they are equally weak. Each of them can occasionally conquer other 'I's, each of them can become Caliph for an hour and then be replaced by another 'I'. None of them can do much good, but almost every one of them, in one hour or even less, can do so much harm that all the other 'I's will have to pay for it all their lives.

Second, although many 'I's do not know one another, they are all closely connected and interdependent, i.e. they all depend on one another without knowing which depends on which.

Here is a general picture of man.

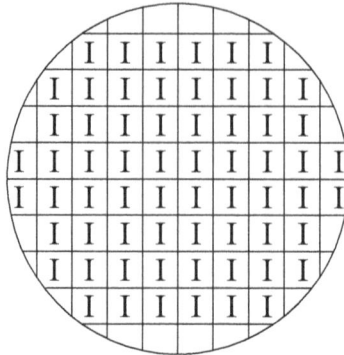

In regard to this diagram and to the interrelation of different 'I's in man, it is very important to understand what follows.

Suppose that two 'I's belonging to different manifestations of a man are connected and he does not know it. Suppose that he does not like one of these 'I's and finds it weak or dangerous. He decides to struggle against it. It may happen that he conquers it, i.e. destroys or weakens it. But by doing this he may, without realizing it, have done something that he did not intend to do and did not even suspect that he was doing. The 'I' that he wanted to destroy was connected with several other 'I's; and in destroying or weakening this 'I' he has, at the same time, destroyed these other 'I's which were connected with the first one—'I's which, by themselves, could have been quite useful.

This refers in particular to habits and to the struggle with those habits which one considers wrong in oneself. A man can sometimes conquer wrong habits but always at the expense of some useful features which are, seemingly, quite unconnected with these habits. In this way a man becomes even more of a slave and even more of a machine than he was before. Therefore, it is much better if a man does not try to do anything, i.e. if he does not try to change and improve himself until he knows himself sufficiently well and knows exactly in what order and in which way things can be changed.

It must be understood that, at every moment of his life, man is a very *well-balanced machine*. 'Balanced' does not mean harmonized or harmonious. There is nothing in the world less harmonious than a man. 'Balanced' means balanced in the sense that if there is one thing in him of which he knows, there is also another, connected with the first, of which, in most cases, he does not know. And the difficulty is that by interfering with one thing he interferes with the other.

Many strange incidents of human life are based on man's unawareness of this balance and his upsetting of it.

Suppose, for instance, that a man notices that he is absent-minded, always forgetting things and so on. He decides to struggle against it and after some time he succeeds; but in a quite unexpected way he becomes miserly and suspicious and finds himself always suspecting people of evil intentions towards him. Or suppose that he finds that he is weak and sentimental about people, always thinking about their sufferings, their helplessness and so on. He begins to struggle with this and develops in himself the desire for domination over people and a complete disregard for their feelings; or suicidal tendencies; or a total loss of all moral values.

Now let us return to these two questions: What does development mean, and what does it mean that man can become a different being or, in other words, what kind of change is possible in man and *how* and *when* does this change begin?

It has already been said that the change will begin with those powers and capacities which man *ascribes to himself,* but which, in reality, he does not possess.

This means that before man can acquire any *new* powers and capacities, he must actually develop in himself those powers and qualities which he ascribes to himself, and about which he has the greatest possible illusions.

Naturally, before such development can begin man must *realize that he does not possess consciousness, individuality, permanent 'I', or will.* Because, so long as he believes that he possesses these qualities, he will not make the right efforts to acquire them, exactly as a man will not buy costly things and pay a high price for them if he thinks that he already possesses them.

The most important and the most misleading of these qualities is consciousness. And the change in man begins with the change in his understanding of the meaning of consciousness and with his acquiring command over it.

What is consciousness?

In most cases in ordinary language, the word 'consciousness' is used as an equivalent to the word 'intelligence' (in the sense of mind activity), or as an alternative for it.

In reality, consciousness is a particular kind of 'awareness' in man, awareness of himself, awareness of who he is, what he feels or thinks, or where he is at the moment. Only man himself can know whether he is 'conscious' at the given moment or not.

But opinions of modern psychological schools differ on the question of consciousness. Some recognize that man is conscious in at least part of his functions; others deny any kind of consciousness in man, deny even the usefulness or the necessity for the term 'consciousness'. I will analyse none of these opinions because, from the point of view of the system about which I speak, they are all wrong. Later, it will become clearer what I mean by this.

For the present I want to draw your attention to three points which have been missed by *all* modern psychological schools.

The first point is that man is not equally conscious all the time, as some systems presume, and he is not equally non-conscious all the time as other systems presume. He is conscious only sporadically and accidentally, and even then only in flashes or for very brief and transitory periods. These sporadic moments of consciousness, plus memory, produce the illusion of contin-uous consciousness.

The second point is that consciousness has definite degrees: (a) in extent and penetration, and (b) in frequency of appear-ance and in duration.

Extent and penetration can be measured by comparing dif-ferent moments of consciousness and their relative value; and frequency and duration can be easily observed and determined as soon as man realizes what he is looking for.

The third point is that consciousness in man can be produced *for a moment* at any time by drawing his attention to it; and, what is really important, that consciousness can be made more or less continuous and permanent by the special efforts and long work on himself of a man desirous of becoming conscious.

The mistakes most commonly made about consciousness are that it is either taken as connected with all manifestations of *intelligence* and inseparable from them, or denied on the basis of the long-established fact that the presence of consciousness cannot be proved by observation of the external actions of man.

I will try to explain how consciousness can be studied.

Take a watch and look at the second hand, trying to be aware of yourself and concentrating on the feeling 'I am So-and-so', 'I am here', and so on. Try not to think about anything else, simply follow the movement of the second hand and be aware of yourself, your name, your existence, the place where you are. Keep all other thoughts away.

You will find, if you are persistent, that you will be able to do this for two minutes. This is the limit of your consciousness. But if you try to repeat the experiment soon after, you will find it more difficult than the first time.

This experiment shows that a man in his natural state can, with great effort, be conscious of *one subject* (himself) for two minutes.

The most important deduction one can make after doing

this experiment in the right way is that man is not conscious of himself. The illusion of his being conscious of himself is created by memory and thought processes. For instance, a man goes to a theatre. If he is accustomed to it, he is not conscious of being there while he is there, although he can see things and observe them, enjoy the performance, remember it and so on. But when he comes back he remembers that he was in the theatre and certainly thinks that he was conscious while he was there. So he has no doubts about his consciousness.

According to the system we are studying, man has the possibility of four states of consciousness. They are: *sleep, waking state, self-consciousness* and *objective consciousness.* But although he has the possibility of these four states of consciousness man actually lives only in two states: one part of his life passes in sleep, and the other part in what is called 'waking state', though in reality it differs very little from sleep.

In ordinary life man knows nothing of 'objective consciousness' and no experiments in this direction are possible. The third state, or 'self-consciousness', he ascribes to himself, i.e. he believes he possesses it, although actually he can be conscious of himself only in very rare flashes, and even then he probably does not recognize it because he does not know what it would imply if he actually possessed it. These glimpses of consciousness come in exceptional moments: in highly emotional states, in moments of danger, in very new and unexpected circumstances and situations; or sometimes in quite ordinary moments when nothing particular happens. But in his ordinary or 'normal' state man has no control of them whatever.

As regards our ordinary memory, or moments of memory, we actually *remember* only moments of consciousness, although we do not see that this is so.

What memory means in a technical sense, I shall explain later. Now I simply want you to turn your attention to your own observations of your memory. You will notice that you remember things differently: some things you remember quite vividly, some very vaguely, and some you do not remember at all. You only *know* that they happened.

This means, for instance, that if you know that some time ago you went to a definite place to speak to someone, you may remember two or three things connected with your conversation with this person; but you may not remember at all how you went there and how you returned. Now, if you are asked if you remember how you went there and how you returned, you will say that you remember distinctly, when, in reality, *you only know it and know where you went; but you do not remember it,* with the exception, possibly, of two or three flashes.

You will be very astonished when you realize how little you actually remember. And it happens in this way because you *remember* only the *moments when you were conscious.* You will understand better what I mean if you try to turn your mind back as far as you can to early childhood, or in any case to something that happened long ago. You will then realize how little you actually remember and how much there is concerning which you simply *know* or *heard that it happened.*

So in reference to the third state of consciousness we can say that man has occasional moments of self-consciousness but he has no command over them. They come and go by themselves, being controlled by external circumstances and occasional associations or emotions.

The question arises: Is it possible to acquire command over these fleeting moments of consciousness, to evoke them more often and to keep them longer, or even make them permanent?

In other words, is it not possible to become conscious?

This is the most important point, and it must be understood at the very beginning of our study that this point has been entirely missed by all modern psychological schools.

For with the right methods and the right efforts man *can* acquire control of consciousness and *can* become fully conscious of himself, with all that it implies; and what it actually implies we, in our present state, do not even imagine.

Only after this point has been understood does a really serious study of psychology become possible.

This study must begin with the investigation of *obstacles* to consciousness in ourselves, because consciousness can only begin to grow when at least some of these obstacles are removed.

In the next lecture I shall speak about these obstacles, the greatest of which is our ignorance in relation to ourselves, and our wrong conviction that we know ourselves, and can be sure of ourselves.

SECOND LECTURE

Further study of states of consciousness. Sleep and awakening. Fallacy of the idea of the subconscious mind. Men living in sleep. Conditions of awakening. Psychological schools. Origin of schools. Necessity for schools for self-development. Psychology as self-study according to school methods. Functions of man. Intellect. Emotions. Instinct. Moving functions. Sex. Two unknown functions which appear only in higher states of consciousness. Study of intellect and emotions. Study of instinctive and moving functions. Their chief difference. Useful and useless functions. Observation of functions in relation to different states of consciousness.

Continuing our study of man, we must now speak with more detail about the different states of consciousness.

As I have already said, there are four states of consciousness possible for man, but he lives only in two. It is as though he had a four-storied house, but lived only in the two lower stories.

The first or the lowest state of consciousness is sleep. This is a purely subjective and passive state. Man is surrounded by dreams. All his psychic functions work without any direction. There is no logic, no sequence, no cause and no result in dreams. Purely subjective pictures—either reflections of former experiences or reflections of vague perceptions of the moment, such as sounds reaching the sleeping man, sensations coming from the body, slight pains, sensation of tension—fly through the mind, leaving only a very slight trace on the memory and more often leaving no trace at all.

The second degree of consciousness comes when man awakes. This second state, the state in which we are now, i.e. in which we work, talk, imagine ourselves conscious beings and so forth, we ordinarily call 'waking consciousness' or 'clear consciousness', but really it should be called 'waking sleep' or 'relative consciousness'. This last term will be explained later.

It is necessary to understand here that the first state of consciousness, i.e. sleep, does not disappear when the second state arrives, i.e. when man awakes. It remains there, with all its dreams and dream impressions, only a more critical attitude towards one's own impressions, more connected thoughts, more disciplined actions become added to it, and because of the vividness of sense impressions, desires, and feelings—particularly the feeling of contradiction or impossibility, which is entirely absent in sleep—dreams become invisible exactly as the stars and moon become invisible in the glare of the sun. But they are all there and they often influence all our thoughts, feelings and actions—sometimes even more than the actual perceptions of the moment.

In connection with this you must bear in mind that I do not mean what is called in modern psychology (or what is known as psychology) 'the subconscious' or 'the subconscious mind'. These are simply wrong expressions, wrong terms, which mean absolutely nothing and do not refer to any real facts. There is nothing subconscious in us because there is nothing conscious; and there is no subconscious mind for the very simple reason that there is no conscious mind. Later you will see how this mistake in regard to the subconscious mind occurred, and how this wrong terminology came into being and became almost generally accepted, at any rate in modern vulgarized forms of psychology.

But let us return to the states of consciousness which really exist. The first is sleep. The second is waking sleep or relative consciousness.

The first, as I have said, is a purely subjective state. The second is less subjective; man already distinguishes 'I' and 'not I' in the sense of his body and objects different from his body, and he can, to a certain extent, orientate among them and know their position and qualities. But it cannot be said that man is awake in this state because he is very strongly influenced by dreams, and really lives more in dreams than in facts. All the absurdities and all the contradictions of people, and of human life in general, become explained when we realize that people *live in sleep,* do everything in sleep, and do not know that they are asleep.

It is useful to remember that this is the inner meaning of many ancient doctrines. The best known to us is Christianity or the Gospel teaching, in which the idea that men live in sleep and must first of all awaken is the basis of all the explanations of human life.

But the question is, *how* can a man awaken?

The Gospel teaching demands awakening but does not say how to awaken.

But the psychological study of consciousness shows that only when a man realizes that he is asleep, is it possible to say that he is on the way to awakening. He never can awaken without first realizing his sleep.

These two states, sleep and relative consciousness or waking sleep, are the only two states of consciousness in which man lives. The two higher states of consciousness are inaccessible to him. He cannot make experiments with them, he cannot know what they are like. They may become accessible to a man only after a hard and prolonged struggle.

The two higher states of consciousness are called 'self-consciousness' and 'objective consciousness'.

We generally think that we are conscious of ourselves, or in any case that we can be conscious of ourselves at any moment we wish, but in truth self-consciousness is a state which *we ascribe to ourselves without any right,* and objective consciousness is a state about which modern psychology knows nothing.

Self-consciousness is a state in which man becomes objective towards himself, and objective consciousness is a state in which he comes into contact with the real or objective world from which he is now shut off by the senses, dreams and subjective states of his so-called consciousness.

Another definition of the four states of consciousness can be made from the point of view of our possible cognition of truth.

In the first state of consciousness, i.e. in sleep, we cannot know anything of the truth. Even if some real perceptions or feelings come to us, they become mixed with dreams, and in the state of sleep we cannot distinguish between dreams and reality.

In the second state of consciousness, i.e. in waking sleep, we can only know *relative* truth, and from this comes the term 'relative consciousness'.

In the third state of consciousness, i.e. in the state of self-consciousness, we can know the full truth *about ourselves*.

In the fourth state of consciousness, i.e. in the state of *objective consciousness,* we are supposed to be able to know the full truth *about everything;* we can study 'things in themselves', 'the world.

This is so far from us that we cannot even think about it in the right way, and we must try to understand that even glimpses of objective consciousness can only come in the fully developed state of self-consciousness.

In the state of sleep we can have glimpses of relative consciousness. In the state of relative consciousness we can have glimpses of self-consciousness. But if we want to have more prolonged periods of self-consciousness and not merely glimpses, we must understand that they cannot come by themselves. They need *will action*. This means that frequency and duration of moments of self-consciousness depend on the command one has over oneself. So it means too that consciousness and will are almost one and the same thing or, in any case, aspects of the same thing.

At this point it must be understood that the first obstacle in the way of the development of self-consciousness in man is his conviction that he already possesses self-consciousness or, at any rate, that he can have it at any time he likes. It is very difficult to persuade a man that he is not conscious, and cannot be conscious, at will. It is particularly difficult because here nature plays a very funny trick.

If you ask a man if he is conscious or if you say to him that he is not conscious, he will answer that he is conscious, and that it is absurd to say that he is not, because he hears and understands you.

And he will be quite right, although at the same time quite wrong. This is nature's trick. He will be right, because your question or your remark has made him vaguely conscious for a moment. Next moment consciousness will disappear. But he will remember what you said and what he answered and he will certainly consider himself conscious.

In reality, acquiring self-consciousness means long and hard work. How can a man agree to this work if he thinks he already possesses the very thing which is promised him as the result of long and hard work? Naturally a man will not begin this work and will not consider it necessary until he becomes convinced that he possesses neither self-consciousness nor all that is connected with it, i.e. unity or individuality, permanent 'I' and will.

This brings us to the question of schools, because methods for the development of *self-consciousness, unity, permanent 'I', and will* can be given only by special schools. That must be clearly understood. Men on the level of relative consciousness cannot find these methods by themselves; and these methods cannot be described in books or taught in ordinary schools for the very simple reason that they are different for different people, and there is no universal method equally applicable to all.

In other words, this means that men who want to change their state of consciousness need a school. But first they must realize their need. As long as they think they can do something by themselves they will not be able to make any use of a school even if they find it. Schools exist only for those who need them, and who know that they need them.

The idea of schools—the study of the kinds of schools that

may exist, the study of school principles and school methods—occupies a very important place in the study of that psychology which is connected with the idea of evolution, because without a school there can be no evolution. One cannot even start, because one does not know how to start: still less can one continue or attain anything.

This means that having got rid of the first illusion that one already has everything one can have, one must get rid of the second illusion that one can get anything by oneself; because by oneself one can get nothing.

These lectures are not a school. A school requires a much higher pressure of work. But in these lectures I can give to those who wish to listen some ideas as to how schools work and how they can be found.

Returning to the study of man, I can now say that psychology really means *self-study*. This is the second definition of psychology. One cannot study psychology as one can study astronomy, i.e. apart from oneself. And one must study oneself as one studies any new and complicated machine. One must know the parts of this machine, its chief functions, the conditions of right work, the causes of wrong work, and many other things which are difficult to describe without using a special language which it is also necessary to know in order to be able to study the machine.

The human machine has seven different functions:
1. Thinking (or intellect).
2. Feeling (or emotions).
3. Instinctive function (all inner work of the organism).
4. Moving function (all outer work of the organism, movement in space and so on).
5. Sex (the function of two principles, male and female, in all their manifestations).

Besides these, there are *two more functions* for which we have no names in ordinary language and which appear only in higher states of consciousness; one in the state of self-consciousness and the other in the state of objective consciousness. As we are not in these states of consciousness we cannot study these functions, and we learn about them only directly or indirectly from those who have attained or experienced them.

In the religious and early philosophical literature of different nations there are many allusions to the higher states of consciousness and to higher functions. What creates an additional difficulty in understanding these allusions is the lack of division between the two higher states of consciousness. What is called *samadhi* or *ecstatic state* or *illumination,* or in more recent works 'cosmic consciousness', is generally described as *one* thing, while in reality these descriptions refer sometimes to moments of self-consciousness and sometimes to moments of objective consciousness, with their corresponding functions. And, strange though it may seem, we have more material for judging the *highest* state, i.e. objective consciousness, than the *intermediate* state, i.e. self-consciousness, although the former may come only *after* the latter.

Self-study must begin with the study of the *four functions:* thinking, feeling, instinctive function and moving function. Sex function can be studied only much later, i.e. when these four functions are already sufficiently understood. Contrary to some modern theories this system regards the sex function as posterior, i.e. as appearing later in life, when the first four functions are already fully manifested, and as being conditioned by them. Therefore the study of the sex function can be useful only when the first four functions are fully known in all their manifestations. At the same time, it must be understood that any serious irregularity or abnormality in the sex function makes self-development, and even self-study, impossible.

So now we must try to understand the four chief functions.

I will take it that it is clear to you what I mean by the thinking function. All mental processes are included here: realization of an impression, formation of representations and concepts, reasoning, comparison, affirmation, negation, formation of words, speech, imagination, pretending, lying and so on.

The second function is feeling or emotions: joy, sorrow, fear, astonishment and so on. Even if you are sure that it is clear to you how, and in what, emotions differ from thoughts, I should advise you to verify all your views in regard to this. We mix thoughts and feelings in our ordinary thinking; but for the beginning of self-study it is necessary to know clearly which is which.

The two following functions, instinctive and moving, will take longer to understand, because in no system of ordinary psychology are these functions described and divided in the right way.

The words 'instinct', 'instinctive' are generally used in the wrong sense and very often in no sense at all. In particular, to instinct are generally ascribed external functions which are, in reality, moving functions, and sometimes emotional.

Instinctive function in man includes in itself:

First. All the inner work of the organism, all physiology, so to speak: digestion and assimilation of food, breathing, circulation of the blood, all the work of inner organs, the building of new cells, the elimination of worked-out materials, the work of glands of inner secretion and so on.

Second. The so-called five senses: sight, hearing, smell, taste, touch, and all other senses such as the sense of weight, of temperature, of dryness or of moisture and so on, i.e. all indifferent sensations, sensations which by themselves are neither pleasant nor unpleasant.

Third. All physical emotions, i.e. all sensations which are either pleasant or unpleasant; all kinds of pain or unpleasant feeling such as unpleasant taste or unpleasant smell, and all kinds of physical pleasure, such as pleasant taste, pleasant smell and so on.

Fourth. All reflexes, even the most complicated, such as laughter and yawning; all kinds of physical memory, such as memory of taste, smell and pain, which are in reality inner reflexes.

Moving function includes in itself all external movements, such as walking, writing, speaking, i.e. production of the voice, eating and so on, i.e. according to ordinary terminology all 'conscious' movements, or movements of which one *can* be aware, and all 'automatic' movements, or movements which are supposed to have been conscious before becoming automatic. To moving function also belong those movements which in ordinary language are called 'instinctive', such as catching a falling object without thinking.

The difference between the instinctive and the moving functions is very clear and can be easily understood if one simply remembers that all instinctive functions without exception are *inherent,* and that there is no necessity to learn them in order to use them; whereas, on the other hand, none of the moving functions are inherent, and one has to learn them all as a child learns to walk, or as one learns to write or to draw or to use a typewriter.

Besides these normal moving functions, there are also some strange moving functions which represent useless work of the human machine not intended by nature, but which occupy a very large place in man's life and waste a great quantity of energy. These are: formation of dreams, imagination, day-dreaming, talking with oneself, all talking for talking's sake and, generally, all uncontrolled and uncontrollable manifestations.

The four functions—intellectual, emotional, instinctive and moving—must first be *understood* in all their manifestations, and later they must be *observed* in oneself. Such self-observation, i.e. observation on the right basis, with a preliminary understanding of the states of consciousness and of different functions, constitutes the basis of self-study, i.e. the beginning of psychology.

It is very important to remember that in observing functions it is useful to observe at the same time their relation to different states of consciousness.

Let us take the three states of consciousness, sleep, waking state or relative consciousness and self-consciousness, and the four functions, thinking, feeling, instinctive and moving. All four functions can manifest themselves in sleep, but their manifestations are desultory and unreliable; they cannot be used in any way, they just go by themselves. In the state of relative consciousness, they can, to a certain extent, serve for our orientation. Their results can be compared, verified, straightened out, and although they may create many illusions, still in our ordinary state we have nothing else and must make of them what we can. If we knew the quantity of wrong observations, wrong theories, wrong deductions and conclusions made in this state, we should cease to believe ourselves altogether. But men do not realize how deceptive their observations and their theories can be, and they continue to believe in them. It is this that keeps men from observing the rare moments when their functions manifest themselves in connection with glimpses of the third state of consciousness or self-consciousness.

All this means that each of the four functions can manifest itself in each of the three states of consciousness. But the results are very different. When we learn to observe these results and their difference, we shall understand the right relation between functions and states of consciousness.

But, before even considering the difference in functions in relation to states of consciousness, it is necessary to understand that man's consciousness and man's functions are quite different phenomena and that one can exist without the other. Functions can exist without consciousness, and consciousness can exist without functions.

THIRD LECTURE

Man's ideas of his possible evolution.   Lack of understanding and discrimination.   Study of lying.   What is lying?   Artificial and real man.   What is born in man and what is acquired by him.   Causes of over-development of personality and under-development of essence.   'Centres' controlling functions.   Relation of 'centres' to essence and personality.   What does it mean to know oneself?   Impossibility of an impartial study of oneself.   Study of useless and harmful functions.   Imagination.   Expression of negative emotions.   Unnecessary talking.   Identification and considering.   Difficulties for self-study and self-knowledge created by our ordinary language.   Necessity of studying a new language.   Principles of the new language.   Seven categories of man.

I n the previous lectures I gave two definitions of psychology. First, I said that psychology is the study of the possible evolution of man, and second, that psychology is the study of oneself.

I meant that only a psychology which investigates the evolution of man is worth studying, and that a psychology which is occupied with only one phase of man without knowing anything about his other phases is obviously not complete and cannot have any value, even in a purely scientific sense, i.e. from the point of view of experiment and observation. For the present phase, as studied by ordinary psychology, in reality does not exist as something separate, and consists of many sub-divisions which lead from lower phases to higher phases. Moreover, the same experiment and observation show that one cannot study psychology as one can study any other science not directly connected with oneself. One has to begin the study of psychology with oneself.

Putting together, first, what we may know about the next phase in the evolution of man, i.e. that it will mean acquiring

25

consciousness, inner unity, permanent ego and will, and second, certain material that we can get by self-observation, i.e. realization of the absence in us of many powers and faculties which we ascribe to ourselves, we come to a new difficulty in understanding the meaning of psychology, and to the necessity for a new definition.

The two definitions given in the previous lectures are not sufficient because man by himself does not know what evolution is possible for him, does not see where he stands at present and ascribes to himself features belonging to higher phases of evolution. In fact, he cannot study himself, being unable to distinguish between the imaginary and the real in himself.

Think for a moment of a caterpillar imagining itself a butterfly, or of an egg imagining itself a bird, or of an acorn imagining itself an oak. The result of these imaginings will be a big caterpillar, a big egg, and a big acorn—and this would be an approximately true picture of representations of a human being imagining his next phase. I say approximately true, because a caterpillar, an egg and an acorn, are comparatively passive beings. They cannot *act* on the basis of their beliefs and imaginings and man can. He can speak, he can write books, he can invent social theories, he can start wars, and all this *on the basis of lying to himself and to others*. The foundation of this lying is the belief in the possibility of a simultaneous and *mechanical* development of *all* human features—which exactly corresponds to the visualization of a big caterpillar, a big egg or a big acorn.

This lying must be exposed before we come to any possibility of the study of truth. So the next definition of psychology must be that psychology is the *study of lying*.

What is lying?

As it is understood in ordinary language, lying means distorting or in some cases hiding the truth, or what people believe to be the truth. This lying plays a very important part in life, but there are much worse forms of lying, when people do not know that they lie. I said in the last lecture that we cannot know the truth in our present state and can only know the truth in the state of objective consciousness. How then can we lie? There seems to be a contradiction here, but in reality there is none. We cannot know the truth but we can pretend that we know. *And this is lying.* Lying fills all our life. People pretend that they know all sorts of things: about God, about the future life, about the universe, about the origin of man, about evolution, about everything, but in reality they do not know anything even about themselves. And every time they speak about something they do not know *as though they knew it,* they lie. Consequently the study of lying becomes of the first importance in psychology.

Psychology is particularly concerned with the lies a man says and thinks about himself. These lies make the study of man very difficult. Man, as he is, is not a genuine article. He is an imitation of something, and a very bad imitation.

Imagine a scientist on some remote planet who has received from the earth specimens of artificial flowers, *without knowing anything about real flowers.* It will be extremely difficult for him to define them—to explain their shape, their colour, the material from which they are made, i.e. wire, cotton-wool and coloured paper—and to classify them in any way.

Psychology stands in a very similar position in relation to man. It has to study an artificial man without knowing the real man.

Obviously, it cannot be easy to study a being such as man who does not himself know what is real and what is imaginary in him. So psychology must begin with a division between the real and the imaginary in man.

It is impossible to study man as a whole, because man is divided into two parts: one part which, in some cases, can be almost *all real,* and the other part which, in some cases, can be almost *all imaginary.* In the majority of ordinary men these two parts are intermixed and cannot easily be distinguished, although they are both there and both have their own particular meaning and effect.

In the system we are studying, these two parts are called *essence* and *personality*.

Essence is what is born with man. Personality is what is acquired. Essence is what is his own. Personality is what is not his own. Essence cannot be lost, cannot be changed or injured as easily as personality. Personality can be changed almost completely with the change of circumstances, it can be lost or easily injured.

If I try to describe what essence is, I must first of all say that it is the basis of man's physical and mental make-up. For instance, one man is naturally what is called a good sailor, another is a bad sailor; one has a musical ear, another has not; one has a capacity for languages, another has not. This is essence.

Personality is all that is *learned* in one or another way, in ordinary language, 'consciously' or 'unconsciously'. In most cases, 'unconsciously' means by imitation which, as a matter of fact, plays a very important part in the building of personality. Even in instinctive functions which naturally should be free from personality, there are usually many so-called 'acquired tastes', i.e. all sorts of artificial likes and dislikes, all of which are acquired by imitation and imagination. These artificial likes and dislikes play a very important and a very disastrous part in man's life. By nature, man should like what is good for him and dislike what is bad for him. But this is so only as long as essence dominates personality as it should dominate it, in other words, when a man is healthy and normal. When personality begins to dominate essence, and when a man becomes less healthy, he begins to like what is bad for him and to dislike what is good for him.

This is connected with the chief thing that can be wrong in the mutual relations of essence and personality.

Normally, essence must dominate personality and then

personality can be quite useful. But if personality dominates essence this produces wrong results of many kinds.

It must be understood that personality is also necessary for man; one cannot live without personality and only with essence. But the growth of essence and personality must be parallel and the one must not outgrow the other.

Cases of essence outgrowing personality may occur among uneducated people. These so-called simple people may be very good and even clever but they are incapable of development in the same way as people with more developed personality. There are different possibilities for them.

Cases of personality outgrowing essence are often to be found among more cultured people and in such cases essence remains in a half-grown or half-developed state.

This means that with a quick and early growth of personality, growth of essence can practically stop at a very early age, and as a result we see men and women externally quite grown-up, but whose essence remains at the age of ten or twelve.

There are many conditions in modern life which greatly favour this under-development of essence. For instance, the infatuation with sport, particularly with games, and sometimes with what is called 'physical culture', can very effectively stop the development of essence, and sometimes at such an early age that essence is never able to recover fully later.

This shows that essence cannot be regarded as connected only with the physical constitution in the simple meaning of the idea. In order to explain more clearly what essence means, I must again return to the study of functions.

I said in the last lecture that the study of man begins with the study of four functions: intellectual, emotional, moving and instinctive. From ordinary psychology and from ordinary thinking, we know that the intellectual functions, thoughts and so on, are controlled or produced by a certain *centre* which we call 'mind' or 'intellect', or more physiologically 'the brain'. And this is quite right. Only, to be really right, we must understand that other functions are also controlled each by its own mind or centre. Thus, from the point of view of the system, there are four minds or centres which control our actions: intellectual mind or centre, emotional mind or centre, moving mind or centre and instinctive mind or centre. In further references to them we shall call them centres. Each centre is quite independent of the others, has its own sphere of action, its own powers and its own ways of development.

Centres, i.e. their structure, capacities, strong sides and defects, belong to essence. Their *contents,* i.e. all that a centre acquires, belong to personality. The contents of centres will be explained later.

As I have already said, personality is as equally necessary for the development of man as is essence, only it must stand in its right place. This is hardly possible because personality is full of wrong ideas about itself. It does not wish to stand in its right place because its right place is secondary and subordinate; and it does not wish to know the truth about itself, for to know the truth will mean abandoning its falsely dominant position and occupying the inferior position which rightly belongs to it.

The wrong relative positions of essence and personality determine the present disharmonious state of man. And the only way to get out of this disharmonious state is by self-knowledge.

To know oneself—this was the first principle and the first demand of old psychological schools. We still remember these words but have lost their meaning. We think that to *know ourselves* means to know our peculiarities, our desires, our tastes, our capacities and our intentions, when in reality it means to know ourselves *as machines,* i.e. to know the structure of one's machine, its parts, the speed of different parts, the conditions governing their work and so on. We realize in a general way that we cannot know any machine without studying it. We must remember this in relation to ourselves and must study our own machines. The means of study is self-observation. There is no other way and no one can do this work for us. We must do it ourselves. But before this we must learn *how* to observe and *what* to observe. I mean, we must understand the technical side of observation: we must know that it is necessary to observe different functions and distinguish between them, remembering at the same time about different states of consciousness, about our sleep and about the many 'I's in us.

Such observation will very soon give results. First of all a man will notice that he cannot observe everything he finds in himself *impartially*. Some things may please him, other things will annoy him, irritate him, even horrify him. And it cannot be otherwise. Man cannot study himself as a remote star or as a curious fossil. Quite naturally he will like in himself what helps his development and dislike what makes his development more difficult, or even impossible. This means that very soon after starting to observe himself, he will begin to distinguish *useful* features and *harmful* features in himself, i.e. useful or harmful from the point of view of his possible self-knowledge, his possible awakening, his possible development. He will see sides of himself which can become conscious, and sides which cannot become conscious and must be eliminated. In observing himself, he must always remember that his self-study is the first step towards his possible evolution.

Now we must see what are those harmful features that man finds in himself.

Speaking in general they are all mechanical manifestations. The first, as has already been said, is *lying*. Lying is necessary in mechanical life. No one can escape it and the more one thinks that one is free from lying, the more one is in it. Life, as it is, could not exist without lying. But from the psychological side, lying has a different meaning. It means speaking about things one does not know and even cannot know, as though one knows and can know.

Not only speaking, even thinking in this way is dangerous, because it creates in man conceit and other attitudes which keep the truth further and further from him. Lying, and particularly lying to oneself, has many hidden and well-disguised forms, and it is necessary to learn to penetrate all these disguises and to discover all the kinds of deceit and self-deceit practised by man.

You must understand that I do not speak from any moral point of view. We have not yet come to questions of what is good and what is bad by itself. I speak only from a practical point of view, of what is useful and what is harmful to self-study and self-development.

Starting in this way, man very soon learns to discover signs by which he can know harmful manifestations in himself. He discovers that the more he can control a manifestation, the less harmful it can be, and that the less he can control it, i.e. the more mechanical it is, the more harmful it can become.

When man understands this he becomes afraid of lying, again not on moral grounds but on the grounds that he cannot control his lying and that lying controls him, i.e. his other functions.

The second dangerous feature he finds in himself is *imagination*. Very soon after starting his observation of himself he comes to the conclusion that the chief obstacle to observation is imagination. He wishes to observe something, but instead of that, imagination starts in him on the same subject, and he forgets about observation. Very soon he realizes that people ascribe to the word imagination a quite artificial and quite undeserved meaning in the sense of *creative or selective faculty*. He realizes that imagination is a *destructive faculty*, that he can *never* control it and that it *always* carries him away from his more conscious decisions, in a direction in which he had no intention of going. Imagination is almost as bad as lying, it is, in fact, lying to oneself. Man starts to imagine something in order to please himself, and very soon he begins to believe what he imagines, or at least some of it.

Further, one finds many very dangerous effects in the *expression of negative emotions*. The term 'negative emotions' means all emotions of violence or depression: self-pity, anger, suspicion, fear, annoyance, boredom, mistrust, jealousy and so on. Ordinarily, one accepts this expression of negative emotions as quite natural and even necessary. Very often people call it 'sincerity'. Of course it has nothing to do with sincerity; it is simply a sign of weakness in man, a sign of bad temper and of incapacity to keep his grievances to himself. Man realizes this when he tries to oppose it. And by this he learns another lesson. He realizes that in relation to mechanical manifestations it is not enough to observe them, it is necessary to resist them, because without resisting them one cannot observe them. They happen so quickly, so habitually and so imperceptibly that one cannot notice them if one does not make sufficient efforts to create obstacles for them.

After the *expression of negative emotions* one notices in oneself or in other people another curious mechanical feature. This is *talking*. There is no harm in talking itself. But with some people, especially with those who notice it least, it really becomes a vice. They talk all the time, everywhere they happen to be, while working, while travelling, even while sleeping. They never stop talking to someone if there is someone to talk to, and if there is no one they talk to themselves.

This too must not only be observed, but resisted as much as possible. With unresisted talking one cannot observe anything and all the results of a man's observations will immediately evaporate in talking.

The difficulties he has in observing these four manifestations— lying, imagination, the expression of negative emotions and unnecessary talking—will show man his utter mechanicalness and the impossibility even of struggling against this mechanicalness without help, i.e. without new knowledge and without actual assistance. For even if a man has received certain material he forgets to use it, forgets to observe himself; in other words, he falls asleep again and again and must always be awakened.

This 'falling asleep' has certain definite features of its own, unknown, or at least unregistered and unnamed, in ordinary psychology. These features need special study.

There are two of them. The first is called *identification*.

'Identifying' or 'identification' is a curious state in which man passes about half of his life, the other half being passed in complete sleep. He 'identifies' with everything: with what he says, what he feels, what he believes, what he does not believe, what he wishes, what he does not wish, what attracts him, what repels him. Everything *becomes him,* or it is better to say *he becomes it.* He becomes all that he likes and all that he dislikes. This means that in the state of identification man is incapable of separating himself from the object of his identification. It is difficult to find the smallest thing with which man is unable to 'identify'. At the same time, in a state of identification man has even less control over his mechanical reactions than at any other time. Such manifestations as lying, imagination, the expression of negative emotions and constant talking *need identification.* They cannot exist without identification. If man *could* get rid of identification, he could get rid of many useless and foolish manifestations.

Identification, its meaning, causes and results, is extremely well described in the *Philokalia* (volume III, Saint Philopheus of Sinai, paragraphs 34-36) which was mentioned in the first lecture. But no trace of understanding of it can be found in modern psychology. It is a quite forgotten 'psychological discovery'.

The second sleep-producing state, akin to identification, is *considering*. Actually, 'considering' is identification with people. It is a state in which man constantly worries about what other people think of him; whether they give him his due, whether they appreciate him enough, whether they like him enough, whether they admire him enough, and so on, and so on. 'Considering' plays a very important part in everyone's life, but in some people it becomes an obsession. All their lives are filled with considering, i.e. worry, doubt and suspicion, and there remains no place for anything else.

The myth of the 'inferiority complex' and other 'complexes' is created by the vaguely realized but not understood phenomenon of 'considering'.

Both 'identifying' and 'considering' must be observed most seriously. Only full knowledge of them can diminish them. If one cannot see them in oneself one can easily see them in other people.

But one must remember that one in no way differs from others. In this sense all people are equal.

Returning now to what was said before, we must try to understand more clearly how the development of man must begin and in what way self-study can help this beginning.

From the very start we meet with a difficulty in our language. For instance, we want to speak about man from the point of view of evolution. But the word 'man' in ordinary language does not admit of any variation or any gradation. Man who is never conscious and never suspects it, man who is struggling to become conscious, man who is fully conscious—it is all the same for our language. It is always 'man' in every case. In order to avoid this difficulty and to help the student in classifying his new ideas, the system divides man into *seven categories*.

The first three categories are practically on the same level.

Man No. 1, a man in whom the moving or instinctive centres predominate over the intellectual and emotional. Physical man.

Man No. 2, a man in whom the emotional centre predominates over the intellectual, moving and instinctive. Emotional man.

Man No. 3, a man in whom the intellectual centre predominates over the emotional, moving and instinctive. Intellectual man.

In ordinary life we meet only these three categories of man. Each one of us and everyone we know is either No. 1, No. 2 or No. 3. There are higher categories of man, but men are not born already belonging to these higher degrees. They are all born No. 1, No. 2 or No. 3, and can reach higher categories only through schools.

Man No. 4 is not born as such. He is a product of school culture. He differs from man No. 1, 2 and 3 by his knowledge of himself, by his understanding of his position and, as it is expressed technically, by his having acquired a permanent centre of gravity. This last means that the idea of acquiring unity, consciousness, permanent 'I' and will, has already become for him more important than his other interests.

It must be added to the characteristics of man No. 4 that his functions and centres are more balanced, in a way in which they could not be balanced without work on himself according to school principles and methods.

Man No. 5 is a man who has acquired *unity* and *self-consciousness*. He is different from ordinary man because in him one of the higher centres already works, and he has many functions and powers that an ordinary man, i.e. man No. 1, 2 and 3 does not possess.

Man No. 6 is a man who has acquired *objective consciousness*. Another higher centre works in him. He possesses many more new faculties and powers beyond the understanding of an ordinary man.

Man No. 7 is a man who has attained all that a man can attain. He has a *permanent 'I'* and *free will*. He can control all the states of consciousness in himself and he already cannot lose anything he has acquired. According to another description, *he is immortal within the limits of the solar system.*

Understanding of this division of man into seven categories is very important, for the division has very many applications in all possible ways of studying human activity. It gives, in the hands of those who understand it, a very strong and very fine weapon for the definition of manifestations which, without it, are impossible to define.

Take, for instance, the general concepts of religion, art, science and philosophy. Beginning with religion we can see at once that there must be a religion of man No. 1, i.e. all forms of fetishism, no matter how they are called; a religion of man No. 2, i.e. emotional, sentimental religion, passing sometimes into fanaticism, the crudest forms of intolerance, persecution of heretics and so on; a religion of man No. 3, i.e. theoretical, scholastic religion, full of argument about words, forms, rituals, which become more important than anything else; a religion of man No. 4, i.e. the religion of a man who works for self-development; a religion of man No. 5, i.e. the religion of a man who has attained unity and can see and know many things that man No. 1, 2 and 3 can neither see nor know; then a religion of man No. 6 and a religion of man No. 7, about neither of which can we know anything.

The same division applies to art, science and philosophy. There must be an art of man No. 1, an art of man No. 2, an art of man No. 3; science of man No. 1, science of man No. 2, science of man No. 3, science of man No. 4 and so on. You must try to find examples of these for yourselves.

This expansion of concepts greatly enlarges our possibility of finding right solutions to many of our problems.

And this means that the system gives us the possibility of studying *a new language,* i.e. new for us, which will connect for us ideas of different categories which are in reality united, and divide ideas of seemingly the same categories which are in reality different. The division of the word 'man' into seven words: Man

No. 1, 2, 3, 4, 5, 6 and 7, with all that follows, is an example of this new language.

This gives us the fourth definition of psychology as *the study of a new language*. And this new language is a *universal language*, which people sometimes try to find or invent.

The expression, 'a universal language', must not be taken in a metaphorical sense. The language is universal in the sense that it includes in itself all that people can know; even the few words of this language which have been explained give you the possibility of thinking and speaking with more precision than is possible in ordinary language.

FOURTH LECTURE

Man as a machine.   The work of centres.   Wrong work of centres.   False idea
of our unity.   Why the human machine works below its normal standard.   Possibility of development of man.   Conditions of development.   What a man
must understand first of all.   Necessity for a school.   Rapid disappearance
of schools.   Ideas from the *Laws of Manu*.   Preparation of man for school
work.   Influences of two kinds under which man lives.   Different results of
different influences.   Formation of a 'magnetic centre'.   New possibilities
for a man opening through magnetic centre.   Facts about schools which one
can learn only in a school.   Three lines of school work.   Study of a school
language.   Impressions and 'material of centres'.   Why one does not see
and does not hear in the state of identification.

T he idea that man is a machine is not a new one. It is really
the only scientific view possible, i.e. a view based on experiment and observation. A very good definition of man's mechanicalness was given in the so-called 'psycho-physiology' of the
second part of the nineteenth century. Man was regarded as
incapable of any movement without receiving external impressions. This idea was connected with the 'theoretical experiment'
as it was then called. Scientists of that time maintained that if it
were possible physically, to deprive man, from birth, of all outer
and inner impressions and still keep him alive, he would not
be able to make the smallest movement, either inner or outer.

Such an experiment is, of course, impossible even with an
animal, because the processes by which life is maintained, breathing, eating and drinking, will produce all sorts of impressions
which will start different reflex movements first and then awaken
the moving centre. But still this idea is interesting because it
shows clearly that the activity of the machine depends on two
things: first, on the kind and quality of external impressions,
and second, on the kind and quality of inner responses.

And here it must be stated very definitely that, apart from useless functions such as lying, imagination, mechanical talk and the rest, and the states of identifying and considering, there are many other aspects of the work of the machine which make the study of it very difficult and which show that the machine does not work at its right level.

Centres in the machine are perfectly adjusted to receive each its own kind of impressions and to respond to them in a corresponding way. And when centres work rightly it is possible to calculate the work of the machine and foresee and foretell many future happenings and responses in the machine, as well as to study them and even direct them. But unfortunately centres, even in what is called a healthy and normal man, very rarely work in exactly the right way.

The cause of this is that centres are made so that, in a certain way, they can replace one another. In the original plan of nature the purpose of this was, undoubtedly, to make the work of centres continuous and to create a safeguard against possible interruptions in the work of the machine, because in some cases an interruption would be fatal.

But the capacity of centres to work for one another in an untrained and undeveloped machine—as all our machines are—becomes excessive and, as a result, the machine only rarely works in the right way. Almost every minute one or another centre leaves its own work and tries to do the work of another centre which in its turn tries to do the work of a third centre.

I said that centres can replace one another in a certain way, but they cannot replace one another completely, and inevitably in such cases their work is much less effective. For instance, the moving centre can, up to a point, continue the work of the intellectual centre, but it can only produce very vague and disconnected thoughts, as for example in dreams and in day-dreaming. In its turn the intellectual centre can work for the moving centre. You can make experiments of this kind by trying to use your mind to do something which your hands or your legs can do without its help, for instance, walking down a staircase noticing every movement, or doing some habitual work with your hands, calculating and preparing every small movement with your mind. You will immediately see how much more difficult the work will become, how much slower and how much more clumsy the intellectual centre is than the moving centre. You can see this also when you *learn* some new kind of movement, such as the use of the typewriter or any kind of physical work. For some time in all your movements you will depend on the intellectual centre. But everyone knows the relief when movements become habitual, when the adjustments become automatic, and when there is no need *to think* and calculate every movement all the time. This means that movement has passed to the moving centre.

The instinctive centre can work for the emotional, and the emotional can occasionally work for all the other centres. And in some cases the intellectual centre has to work for the instinctive centre, although it can only do a very small part of its work, the part which is connected with visible instinctive movements, such as the movement of the chest during breathing. It is very dangerous to interfere with the normal functions of the instinctive centre, as for instance, to practise what is sometimes described as Yoga breathing. Breathing exercises of this kind must never be undertaken without the advice and observation of a competent and experienced teacher.

Returning to the wrong work of centres, I must say that, even without intentional interference with them, this wrong work fills up practically our whole life. Our dull impressions, our vague impressions, our lack of impressions, our slow understanding of many things, very often our identifying and our considering, even our lying, all these depend on the wrong work of centres. The idea of the wrong work of centres does not enter into our ordinary thinking and ordinary knowledge, and we do not realize how much harm it does to us, how much energy we spend unnecessarily in this way and the difficulties into which this wrong work of centres leads us.

Insufficient understanding of the wrong work of our machine is usually connected with the false notion of our unity. When we understand how much we are divided in ourselves, we begin to realize the danger that can lie in the fact that one part of ourselves works instead of another part, without our knowing it.

In the way of self-study and self-observation it is necessary to study and observe not only the right work of centres, but also the wrong work of centres. It is necessary to know all kinds of wrong work and the particular features of wrong work belonging to particular individuals. It is impossible to know oneself without knowing one's defects and wrong features. In addition to general defects belonging to everyone, each of us has his own particular defects belonging only to himself, and these too have to be studied at the right time.

I pointed out at the beginning of this lecture that the idea that man is a machine brought into motion by external influences is really and truly a scientific idea.

What science does not know is: first, that the human machine does not work up to its standard, and actually works much below its normal standard, i.e. not with its full powers, not with all its parts; and second, that in spite of this, and in spite of many other things, it is capable of developing and creating for itself quite different standards of receptivity and action.

We shall now speak about the conditions necessary for development because it must be remembered that although development is possible, it is at the same time very rare and requires a great number of external and internal conditions.

The first is that a man must understand his position, his difficulties and his possibilities and must have either a very strong desire to get out of his present state or a very strong inclination for the new, for the unknown state which must come with the change. In short, he must be either very strongly repelled by his present state or very strongly attracted by the future state that may be attained.

The second is that a man must have an adequate preparation. He must learn many new things, and he must be able to understand what he is told.

The third is that a man must be in a suitable position, he must have sufficient free time for study and must live in circumstances which make such study practicable. Besides that, he must be essentially a 'normal man', i.e. he must be free from the different mental and physical kinks which are often taken as originality.

But it is impossible to enumerate all the conditions which are necessary. They include among other things a school. And 'school' implies such social and political order in the given country that a school is possible there, because a school cannot exist in *any* social order. A more or less arranged life, a definite level of culture and a certain amount of personal freedom for everyone are necessary for the existence of a school. Our time is particularly difficult in this respect. Schools in Europe disappeared long ago: schools in the East are disappearing very rapidly. In many countries the existence of schools is simply not possible. For instance, no school can exist in Bolshevik Russia, or in Hitler's Germany, or in Mussolini's Italy.

I quoted in *A New Model of the Universe,* some verses from the *Laws of Manu* referring to this question of the relation of esoteric work to the state of things in life.

Chapter IV.

From *the rules for a Snataka [householder]*:

61.   He must not live in a country governed by Sudras, nor in one inhabited by impious men, nor in one conquered by heretics, nor in one abounding with men of lower castes.

79.   He must not be in the company of outcasts, nor of Kandalas, nor of Pukkasas, nor of idiots, nor of arrogant men, nor of men of low class, nor of Antyavasayins [grave-diggers].

Chapter VIII.

22. A kingdom peopled mostly by Sudras, filled with godless men and deprived of twice-born inhabitants, will soon wholly perish, stricken by hunger and disease.

These ideas from the *Laws of Manu* are very interesting because they give us a basis on which we can judge the real value of one or another social order from the point of view of school work; they enable us to see whether an order is really progressive or only destructive—although supporters of it may assert that it is progressive and even manage to deceive large numbers of weak-minded people.

But all external conditions do not depend on us. To a certain extent, and sometimes with great difficulty, we can choose the country where we prefer to live, but we cannot choose the period or the century, and must try to find what we want in the period in which we are placed by fate.

Here we are faced with another difficulty. Even civilized countries can be attacked by their more barbarous neighbours or in some other way become entangled in war. Conditions of war-time make school work impossible. It may be said that wars are and always have been the chief obstacle to the existence and growth of schools and to the spread of esoteric knowledge. Most schools that have existed, from the time of the ancient mysteries to the present time, have been destroyed by wars or have disappeared during wars. It sounds almost paradoxical but another obstacle to the spread of school teachings can be found in the various intellectual theories such as pacifism, 'non-resistance to evil', all 'non-violence' campaigns and so forth which, for some hidden reason, invariably lead to the annihilation of all the natural safeguards of cultured life and provoke different kinds of destructive emotions and activities which are hostile to peace, despite all protestations of their adherents to the contrary.

So we must understand that even the beginning of preparation for development needs a combination of external and internal conditions which only rarely come all together.

But at the same time we must understand that, at least so far as internal conditions are concerned, a man is not left entirely to the law of accident. There are many lights arranged for him by which he can find his way if he cares to and if he is *lucky*. His possibility is so small that the element of *luck* cannot be excluded.

Let us now try to answer the question: What makes man desire to acquire new knowledge and to change himself?

Man lives in life under *influences of two kinds*. This must be very well understood and the difference between the two kinds of influence must be very clear.

The first kind consists of interests and attractions created in *life itself;* interests of one's health, safety, wealth, pleasures, amusements, security, vanity, pride, fame and so on.

The second kind consists of interests of a different order, aroused by ideas which are not created in life but come originally from schools. These influences do not reach man directly. They are thrown into the general circulation of life, pass through many different minds and reach a man through philosophy, science, religion and art, always mixed with influences of the first kind and generally very little resembling what they were in their origin. In most cases men do not realize the different origin of these influences and often explain them as having the same origin as the first kind.

Although man may not know of the existence of these two kinds of influence, they both act on him and in one or another way he responds to them.

He can be more impressed with one or with some of the influences of the first kind and not feel influences of the second kind at all. Or he can be attracted and affected by one or another of the influences of the second kind. The result is different in each case.

We shall call the first kind, influences *a,* and the second kind, influences *b.*

If a man is fully in the power of influences *a,* or of one particular influence *a,* and quite indifferent to influences *b,* nothing happens to him and his possibility of development diminishes with every year of his life, and at a certain age, sometimes quite an early age, it disappears completely. This means that a man dies while physically he remains still alive, like a grain that cannot germinate and produce a plant.

But if, on the other hand, a man is not completely in the power of influences *a* and if influences *b* attract him and make him feel and think, *the results of the impressions they produce accumulate in him,* attract other influences of the same kind and grow, occupying a more and more important place in his mind and life.

If the results produced by influences *b* become sufficiently strong, they fuse together and form in a man what is called a 'magnetic centre'. It must be understood at once that the word 'centre' in this case has not the same meaning as centres in the organism—the intellectual, emotional, moving and instinctive centres—i.e. centres in the essence. 'Magnetic centre' is in personality, and it is simply a group of interests which, when they become sufficiently strong, serve, to a certain degree, as a guiding and a controlling factor. 'Magnetic centre' turns one's attention in a certain direction and helps to keep it there. At the same time it cannot do much by itself. A school is necessary. 'Magnetic centre' cannot replace a school, but it can help one to realize the need of a school, it can help one to begin to look for a school, or if one meets a school by chance 'magnetic centre' can help one to recognize a school and try not to lose it. For nothing is easier to lose than a school.

Possession of a magnetic centre is the first, although quite unspoken, demand of a school. If a man without a magnetic centre, or with a small or weak magnetic centre, or with several contradictory magnetic centres interested in many incompatible things at the same time, meets a school, he does not become interested in it, or he at once becomes critical before he can learn anything, or his interest disappears very quickly when he meets with the first difficulties of school work. This is the chief safeguard of a school. Without it the school would be filled with people of quite a wrong kind who would immediately distort the school teaching. A right magnetic centre helps one not only to recognize a school, but also to absorb the school teaching, which is different from both influences *a* and influences *b* and may be called influence *c*. Influence *c* can be transferred only by word of mouth, by direct instruction, explanation and demonstration.

When a man meets with influence *c* and is able to absorb it, it may be said of him that in one point of himself, i.e. in magnetic centre, he becomes free from the law of accident. From this moment magnetic centre has actually played its part. It has brought a man to a school and helped him in his first steps there. From then on the ideas and the teaching of the school take the place of the magnetic centre and slowly begin to penetrate into the different parts of personality and, with time, into essence.

One can learn many things about schools, about their organization and their activity, in the ordinary way by reading and by studying historical periods when schools were more conspicuous and more accessible as, for instance, the periods when the mysteries existed in Egypt, in Greece and in other countries. But there are certain things about schools that one can learn only in schools themselves. And the explanation of school principles and rules occupies a very considerable place in school teaching.

One of the most important principles which is learned in this way is that real school work must proceed *by three lines simultaneously*. One line of work, or two lines of work, cannot be called real school work.

What are these three lines?

In the second lecture I said that these lectures are not a school. Now I shall be able to explain why they are not a school.

Once at a lecture a question was asked: Do people who study this system work only for themselves or do they work for other people? Now I shall answer this question.

The first line of school work is study of oneself and study of the system, or the 'language'. Working on this line one certainly works for *oneself.*

The second line is work *with other people* in the school and, working with them, one works not only with them but *for* them. So in the second line one learns to work with people and for people.

The third line is work *for the school.* In order to work for the school one must first understand the work of the school, understand its aims and needs. And this requires time and study— although it happens occasionally that some people come already sufficiently prepared in a certain way. In this case they can begin very soon on the third line, i.e. they can make themselves useful to the school from the very beginning of their study.

The second line is particularly difficult for some people. Very often I hear people say that they have nothing against the system or *even against me,* but the awful thing for them is that they have to work with the group and particularly with 'these people'. 'These people' means all other people besides themselves. And they themselves in their turn are 'these people' for others.

When I said that these lectures are not a school, I meant that these lectures give the possibility of only one line of work, i.e. study of the system and self-study. It is true that even by learning together people study the beginning of the second line of work; at least they learn to *bear one another,* and if their thought is broad enough and their perception quick enough they can even grasp something about the second and third lines of work. Still one cannot expect much from lectures alone.

In the second line of work people must not only *talk* together, but *work* together. This work can be very different but it should always, in one or another way, *be useful to the school.* So it means that working on the first line people study the second line, and working on the second line they study the third line. Later you will learn why three lines of work are necessary and why only three lines can proceed successfully and towards a definite aim.

Even now you can understand the necessity for three lines of work if you realize that man is asleep and that, whatever work he starts, he soon loses interest in it and continues it mechanically. Mechanical work cannot lead anywhere.

Three lines of work are necessary, because one line awakens a man who falls asleep over another line. If one really works on three lines one can never fall asleep completely; one will always awaken and realize that one's work has stopped.

I can indicate also a very characteristic difference between the three lines of work.

In the first line one works chiefly on the study of the system and on self-study, and one must show in one's work a certain amount of initiative.

In the second line one works in connection with a certain organized work and one must only do what one is told. No initiative is required or admitted in the second line and the chief point in this line is to obey and to do exactly what one is told, without bringing in any of one's own ideas even if they seem better than those that have been given.

In the third line one can again show much initiative, but one must always verify oneself and not let oneself make decisions against rules and principles, or against what one has been told.

I have already said that the work begins with the study of the language. It will be very useful if at this point you try to realize that you already know a certain number of words of this new language, and it will also be very useful if you try to count these new words and write them down together. Only they must be written down without comments, i.e. without any interpretation. Comments and interpretations or explanations must be in your understanding; you cannot put them on paper. If this were possible, the study of esoteric teachings would be very simple. It would be sufficient to publish a sort of dictionary or glossary and people would know all that it is necessary to know. But, fortunately or unfortunately, this is impossible and each man has to learn and work for himself.

We must again return to centres and find the reason why we cannot develop more quickly without a long period of school work.

We know that when we learn something we accumulate new material in our memory. But what is our memory? And what is new material? To understand this, we must learn to regard each centre as a separate and independent machine, consisting of a sensitive matter which, by its function, is similar to the matter from which phonographic rolls are made. All that happens to us, all that we see, all that we hear, all that we feel, all that we learn is registered on these rolls. This means that all external and internal events leave certain impressions on the rolls. 'Impressions' is a very good word because they actually are *impressions or imprints* that are left. An impression can be deep, or it can be slight, or it can be simply a glancing impression that disappears very quickly and leaves no trace behind it. But whether deep or slight it is an impression. And these impressions on rolls are all that we have, all our possessions. Everything that we know, everything that we have learned, everything that we have experienced is all there on our rolls. Exactly in the same way all our thought-processes, calculations and speculations consist only of comparing the inscriptions on rolls, reading them again and again, trying to understand them by putting them together and so on. We can think of nothing new, nothing that is not on our rolls. We can neither say nor do anything that does not correspond to some inscription on the rolls. We cannot invent a new thought just as we cannot invent a new animal, because all our ideas of animals are created from our observation of existing animals.

Inscriptions or impressions on rolls are connected by associations. Associations connect impressions either received simultaneously or in some way similar to one another.

In the first lecture I said that memory depends on consciousness and that we actually remember only the moments when we had flashes of consciousness. It is quite clear that different simultaneous impressions connected together will remain longer in the memory than unconnected impressions. In the flash of self-consciousness, or even near to it, all the impressions of the moment are connected and remain connected in the memory. The same applies to impressions connected by their inner similarity. If one is more conscious at the moment of receiving impressions, one more definitely connects the new impressions with similar old impressions and they remain connected in the memory. On the other hand, if one receives impressions in a state of identification, one simply does not notice them and their traces disappear before they can be appreciated or associated. In the state of identification, one does not see and one does not hear; one is wholly in one's grievance, or in one's desire, or in one's imagination. One cannot separate oneself from things or feelings or memories and one is shut off from all the world around.

FIFTH LECTURE

A diagram of centres. Speed of centres. Study of the speeds of functions. Different time in different centres. Phenomena inexplicable for ordinary physiology. Inner divisions of centres and their functions. Divisions in the intellectual and instinctive centres. Positive and negative parts of centres. Affirmation and negation. Pleasant and unpleasant sensations. Divisions in the emotional centre. Unexpected realizations. Positive and negative emotions. How can positive emotions be defined? Positive emotions impossible for man in his present state. Predominance of negative emotions. What creates negative emotions. Identification and imagination. The truth about negative emotions. Man must sacrifice his suffering. Origin of negative emotions. The only good thing in our present state. What one discovers in observing oneself. Possibility of self-remembering.

We shall begin today with a more detailed examination of centres. This is the diagram of four centres.

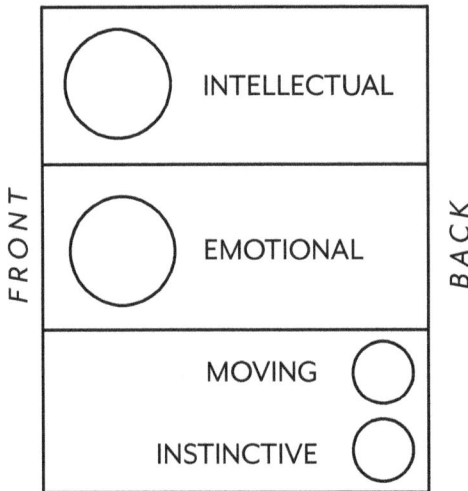

The diagram represents a man standing sideways looking to

the left, and indicates the relative position of centres in a very schematic way.

In reality each centre occupies the whole body, penetrates, so to speak, the whole organism. At the same time, each centre has what is called its 'centre of gravity'. The centre of gravity of the intellectual centre is in the brain; the centre of gravity of the emotional centre is in the solar plexus; the centres of gravity of the moving and instinctive centres are in the spinal cord. The diagram refers to those centres of gravity.

It must be understood that in the present state of scientific knowledge we have no means of verifying this statement, chiefly because each centre includes in itself many traits which are still unknown to existing physiology *and even to anatomy.* It may sound strange, but the fact is that the anatomy of the human body is far from being a completed science.

So the study of centres, which are hidden from us, must begin with the observation of their functions, which are quite open for our investigation.

This is quite a usual course. In the different sciences—physics, chemistry, astronomy, physiology—when we cannot reach the facts we wish to study, we have to begin with an investigation of their results or traces. In this case we shall be dealing with the direct functions of centres; so all that we establish about functions can be applied to centres.

You may ask: Have centres been seen? Can their existence be proved ? How, without this proof, can we speak about them as if they were facts when actually no one knows anything about them?

But it is very easy to reply to such questions. In scientific investigation one very often deals with things which no one has seen and probably never will see. For instance, has anyone seen molecules?

Has anyone seen atoms? Has anyone seen electrons? Yet we take them as facts and base our theories and deductions on them because their existence is proved by the results of their existence. Equally so, by a further investigation and study of the functions of centres and their differences, doubts as to the actual existence of centres themselves become quite futile and unnecessary.

All centres have much in common and, at the same time, each centre has its own peculiar characteristics which must always be kept in mind.

One of the most important principles that must be understood in relation to centres is the great difference in their speed, i.e. a difference in the speeds of their functions.

The slowest is the intellectual centre. Next to it—although very much faster—stand the moving and instinctive centres, which have more or less the same speed. The fastest of all is the emotional centre, though in the state of 'waking sleep' it works only very rarely with anything approximating to its real speed, and generally works with the speed of the instinctive and moving centres.

Observations can help us to establish a great difference in the speeds of functions, but they cannot give us the exact figures. In reality the difference is very great, greater than one can imagine as being possible between functions of the same organism. As I have just said, with our ordinary means we cannot calculate the difference in the speed of centres, but, if we are told what it is, we can find many facts which will confirm not the figures but the existence of the enormous difference.

So before bringing in figures, I want to speak about the ordinary observations which can be made without any special knowledge.

Try, for instance, to compare the speed of mental processes with moving functions. Try to observe yourself when you have to do many quick simultaneous movements, as when driving a car in a very crowded street, or riding fast on a bad road, or doing any work requiring quick judgment and quick movements. You will see at once that you cannot observe all your movements. You will either have to slow them down or miss the greater part of your observations; otherwise you will risk an accident and probably have one if you persist in observing. There are many similar observations which can be made, particularly on the emotional centre which is still faster. Everyone of us really has many observations of the different speeds of our functions, but only very rarely do we know the value of our observations and experiences. Only when we know the principle do we begin to understand our own previous observations.

At the same time it must be said that all the figures referring to these different speeds are established and known in school systems. As you will see later, the difference in the speed of centres is a very strange figure which has a cosmic meaning, i.e. it enters into many cosmic processes or it is better to say it divides many cosmic processes one from another. This figure is 30,000. This means that the moving and instinctive centres are 30,000 times faster than the intellectual centre. And the emotional centre, when it works with its proper speed, is 30,000 times faster than the moving and instinctive centres.

It is difficult to believe in such an enormous difference in the speeds of functions in the same organism. It actually means that different centres have a quite *different time*. The instinctive and moving centres have 30,000 times longer time than the intellectual centre, and the emotional centre has 30,000 times longer time than the moving and instinctive centres.

Do you understand clearly what 'longer time' means? It means that for every kind of work that a centre has to do, it has so much more time. However strange it may be, this fact of the great difference in the speed of centres explains many well-known phenomena which ordinary science cannot explain and which it generally passes over in silence, or simply refuses to discuss. I am referring now to the astonishing and quite inexplicable speed of some of the physiological and mental processes.

For instance, a man drinks a glass of brandy, and *immediately,* in no more than a second, he experiences many new feelings and sensations: warmth, relaxation, relief, peace, contentment, well-being, or perhaps, anger, irritation and so on. These feelings may change, but the fact remains that the body responds to the stimulant *very quickly,* almost at once.

There is really no need to speak about brandy or any other stimulant; if a man is very thirsty or very hungry, a glass of water or a piece of bread will produce the same quick effect.

Similar phenomena representing the enormous speed of certain processes can be noticed, for instance, in observing dreams. I referred to some of these observations in *A New Model of the Universe.*

The difference is again either between the instinctive and the intellectual centres or between the moving and the intellectual. But we are so accustomed to these phenomena that we rarely think how strange and incomprehensible they are.

Of course, for a man who has never thought about himself and never tried to study himself, there is nothing remarkable in this or in anything else. But in reality, from the point of view of scientific physiology, these phenomena look almost miraculous.

A physiologist knows how many complicated processes must be gone through between swallowing brandy and feeling its effects. And all this happens in one second or less. It is a miracle, and at the same time it is not. For if we know the difference in the speed of centres and remember that the instinctive centre, which has to do this work, has 30,000 times more time than the intellectual centre by which we measure our ordinary time, we can understand how it may happen. It means that the instinctive centre has not one second, but *about eight hours* of its time for this work, and in eight hours this work can certainly be done in an ordinary laboratory without any unnecessary haste. So our idea of the extraordinary speed of this work is purely an illusion which we have because we think that our ordinary time, or the time of the intellectual centre, is the only time which exists.

We shall return later on to the study of the difference in speed of centres.

Now we must try to understand another characteristic of centres which will later give us very good material for self-observation and for work upon ourselves.

It is supposed that each centre is divided into two parts, positive and negative.

This division is particularly clear in the intellectual centre and in the instinctive centre.

All the work of the intellectual centre is divided into two parts: *affirmation* and *negation; yes* and *no*. In every moment of our thinking, either one outweighs the other or they come to a moment of equal strength which results in indecision. The negative part of the intellectual centre is as useful as the positive part, and any diminishing of the strength of the one in relation to the other results in mental disorders.

In the work of the instinctive centre the division is also quite clear, and both parts, positive and negative or pleasant and unpleasant, are equally necessary for a right orientation in life.

Pleasant sensations of taste, smell, touch, temperature—warmth, coolness, fresh air—all indicate conditions which are beneficial for life; and unpleasant sensations of bad taste, bad smell, unpleasant touch, feeling of oppressive heat or extreme cold, all indicate conditions which can be harmful for life.

It may definitely be said that no true orientation in life is possible without both pleasant and unpleasant sensations. They are the real guidance of all organic life on the earth, and any defect in them results in a lack of orientation and the consequent danger of illness and death. Think how quickly a man will poison himself if he loses all sense of taste or smell, or if he 'conquers' in himself a natural disgust of unpleasant sensations.

In the moving centre, the division into two parts, positive and negative, has only a logical meaning, i.e. movement as opposed to rest. It has no meaning for practical observation.

In the emotional centre, at a first glance, the division is quite simple and obvious. If we take pleasant emotions such as joy, sympathy, affection, self-confidence, as belonging to the positive part, and unpleasant emotions such as boredom, irritation, jealousy, envy, fear, as belonging to the negative part, things will look very simple; but in reality they are much more complicated.

To begin with, in the emotional centre there is no natural negative part. The greater part of negative emotions are artificial; they do not belong to the emotional centre proper and are based on instinctive emotions which are quite unrelated to them but are transformed by imagination and identification. This is the real meaning of the theory of James and Lange. According to this theory, all these emotions are really sensations of changes in inner organs and tissues, changes which take place before sensations, and are the actual cause of sensations. That really means that external events and inner realizations do not produce emotions. External events and inner realizations produce inner reflexes which produce sensations; and these are interpreted as emotions.

At the same time, positive emotions such as 'love', 'hope', 'faith', in the sense in which they are usually understood, i.e. as permanent emotions, are impossible for a man in the *ordinary* state of consciousness. These emotions require higher states of consciousness; they require inner unity, self-consciousness, permanent 'I' and will. *Positive emotions are emotions which cannot become negative.* But all our pleasant emotions such as joy, sympathy, affection, self-confidence can, at any moment, turn into boredom, irritation, envy, fear and so on. Love can turn into jealousy or fear of losing what one loves, or into anger and hatred; hope can turn into day-dreaming and the expectation of impossible things, and faith can turn into superstition and a weak acceptance of comforting nonsense.

Even such emotions as a purely intellectual emotion, i.e. the desire for knowledge, or an aesthetic emotion, i.e. a feeling of beauty or harmony, if they become mixed with identification, immediately unite with emotions of a negative kind such as self-pride, vanity, selfishness, conceit and so on.

So we can say without any possibility of mistake that we can have no positive emotions. At the same time, in actual fact, we have no negative emotions which exist without imagination and identification. Of course it cannot be denied that, besides the many and varied kinds of physical suffering which belong to the instinctive centre, man has many kinds of mental suffering which belong to the emotional centre. He has many sorrows, griefs, fears, apprehensions and so on which cannot be avoided and are as closely connected with man's life as illness, pain and death. But these mental sufferings are very different from negative emotions which are based on imagination and identification.

These negative emotions are a terrible phenomenon. They occupy an enormous place in our life. Of many people it is possible to say that all their lives are regulated and controlled, and in the end ruined, by *negative emotions*. At the same time, negative emotions do not play any useful part at all in our lives. They do not help our orientation, they do not give us any knowledge, they do not guide us in any sensible manner. On the contrary, they spoil all our pleasures, they make life a burden to us and they very effectively prevent our possible development *because there is nothing more mechanical in our life than negative emotions*.

Negative emotions can never come under our control. People who think they can control their negative emotions and manifest them when they want to, simply deceive themselves. Negative emotions depend on identification; if identification is destroyed in some particular case, they disappear. The strangest and most fantastic fact about negative emotions is that people actually worship them.

I think that, for an ordinary mechanical man, the most difficult thing to realize is that his own and other people's negative emotions have no value whatever and *do not contain anything noble, anything beautiful or anything strong.* In reality negative emotions contain nothing but weakness and very often the beginning of hysteria, insanity or crime. The only good thing about them is that, being quite useless and artificially created by imagination and identification, they can be destroyed without any loss. And this is the only chance of escape that man has.

If negative emotions were useful or necessary for any, even the smallest, purpose, and if they were a function of a really existing part of the emotional centre, man would have no chance, because no inner development is possible so long as man keeps his negative emotions.

In school language it is said on the subject of the struggle with negative emotions: *Man must sacrifice his suffering.*

'What could be easier to sacrifice?' everyone will say. But in reality people will sacrifice anything rather than their negative emotions. There is no pleasure and no enjoyment man will not sacrifice for quite small motives but he will never sacrifice his suffering. And in a sense there is a reason for this.

Many people have nothing but negative emotions. All their 'I's are negative. If you take negative emotions away from them, they simply collapse and go up in smoke.

And what would happen to all our life without negative emotions? What would happen to what we call art, to the theatre, to drama, to most novels?

Unfortunately there is no chance of negative emotions disappearing. Negative emotions can be conquered and can disappear only with the help of school knowledge and school methods. The struggle against negative emotions is a part of school training and is closely connected with all school work.

What is the origin of negative emotions if they are artificial, unnatural and useless? As we do not know the origin of man we cannot discuss this question, and we can speak about negative emotions and their origin only in relation to ourselves and our lives. For instance, in watching children we can see how they are *taught negative emotions* and how they *learn* them themselves through imitation of grown-up people and older children.

If, from the earliest days of his life, a child could be put among people who have no negative emotions, he would probably have none, or so very few that they could be easily conquered by education. But in actual life things happen quite differently, and with the help of all the examples he can see and hear, with the help of reading, the cinema and so on, a child of about ten already knows the whole scale of negative emotions and can reproduce them and identify with them as well as any grown-up man.

In grown-up people negative emotions are supported by the constant justification and glorification of them in literature and art, and by personal self-justification and self-indulgence. Even when we become tired of them we do not believe that we can become quite free from them.

In reality, we have much more power over negative emotions than we think, particularly when we already know how dangerous they are and how urgent is the struggle with them. But we find too many excuses for them, and swim in the seas of self-pity and selfishness, as the case may be, finding fault in everything except ourselves.

All that has just been said shows that we are in a very strange position in relation to our emotional centre. It has no positive part and no negative part. Most of its negative functions are invented, and there are many people who have never in their lives experienced any *real* emotion, so completely is their time occupied with imaginary negative emotions. So we cannot say that our emotional centre is divided into two parts, positive and negative. We can only say that we have pleasant emotions and unpleasant emotions, and that all of them which are not negative at a given moment *can turn into negative emotions under the slightest provocation or even without any provocation.*

This is the true picture of our emotional life and if we look sincerely at ourselves we must realize that so long as we keep in ourselves all these poisonous emotions we cannot expect to be able to develop *unity, consciousness or will.* If such development were possible, then all these imaginary negative emotions would enter into our new being and become permanent in us. This would mean that it would be impossible for us ever to get rid of them. Luckily for us, such a thing cannot happen.

In our present state the only good thing about us is that there is nothing permanent in us. If anything becomes permanent in a man in our present state, it means insanity. Only lunatics can have a permanent ego.

Incidentally this fact disposes of another false term that has crept into the psychological language of the day from the so-called psychoanalysis: I mean the word 'complex'.

There is nothing in our psychological make-up that corresponds to the idea of 'complex'. In the psychiatry of the nineteenth century, what is now called a 'complex' was called a 'fixed idea', and 'fixed ideas' were taken as signs of insanity. And that remains perfectly correct. A normal man cannot have 'fixed ideas','complexes' or 'fixations'. It is useful to remember this in case someone tries to find complexes in you. We have many bad features as it is and our chances are very small even without complexes.

Returning now to the question of work on ourselves we must ask ourselves what our chances actually are. We must discover in ourselves functions and manifestations which we can, to a certain extent, control, and we must exercise this control, trying to increase it as much as possible. For instance, we have a certain control over our movements, and in many schools, particularly in the East, work on oneself begins with acquiring as full a control over movements as possible. But this needs special training, very much time and the study of very elaborate exercises. Under the conditions of modern life we have more control over our thoughts, and in connection with this there is a special method by which we may work on the development of our consciousness using that instrument which is most obedient to our will, i.e. our *mind,* or the intellectual centre.

In order to understand more clearly what I am going to say, you must try to remember that we have no control over our consciousness. When I said that we can become more conscious, or that a man can be made conscious for a moment simply by asking him if he is conscious or not, I used the words 'conscious' or 'consciousness' in a relative sense. There are so many degrees of consciousness and every higher degree means more 'conscious' in relation to a lower degree. But, if we have no control over consciousness itself, we have a certain control over our thinking about consciousness, and we can construct our thinking in such a way as to bring consciousness. What I mean is that by giving to our thoughts a direction which they would have in a moment of consciousness, we can, in this way, induce consciousness.

Now try to formulate what you noticed when you tried to observe yourself.

You noticed three things. First, that you do not *remember yourself,* i.e. that you are not aware of yourself at the time when you try to observe yourself. Second, that observation is made difficult by the incessant stream of thoughts, images, echoes of conversation, fragments of emotions flowing through your mind and very often distracting your attention from observation. And third, that the moment you start self-observation something in you starts imagination, and self-observation—if you really tried it—is a constant struggle with imagination.

Now this is the chief point in work upon oneself. If one realizes that all the difficulties in the work depend on the fact that one cannot *remember oneself,* one already knows what one must do.

One must try to remember oneself.

In order to do this one must struggle with mechanical thoughts and one must struggle with imagination.

If one does this conscientiously and persistently one will see results in a comparatively short time. But one must not think that it is easy or that one can master this practice immediately. *Self-remembering,* as it is called, is a very difficult thing to learn to practise. It must not be based on an expectation of results, otherwise one can identify with one's own efforts. It must be based on the realization of the fact that we do not remember ourselves, and that at the same time we *can* remember ourselves, if we try sufficiently hard and in the right way.

We cannot become conscious at will, at the moment when we want to, because we have no command over states of consciousness. But we can *remember ourselves* for a short time at will, because we have a certain command over our thoughts. And if we start remembering ourselves by the special construction of our thoughts, i.e. by the realization that we do not remember ourselves, that no one remembers himself, and by realizing what it means, this will bring us to consciousness.

You must understand that we have found the weak spot in the wall of our mechanicalness. This is the knowledge that we do not remember ourselves and the realization that we can try to remember ourselves. Up to this moment our task has only been self-study. Now, with the understanding of the necessity for actual change in ourselves, work begins.

Later on you will learn that the practice of self-remembering, connected with self-observation and with the struggle against imagination, has not only a psychological meaning, but it also changes the subtlest part of our metabolism and produces definite chemical, or perhaps it is better to say alchemical, effects in our body. So today, from psychology we have come to alchemy, i.e. to the idea of the transformation of coarse elements into finer ones.

SIXTH LECTURE

Two lines of development of man: knowledge and being.   An idea forgotten in modern thought.   What does understanding mean?   An example of a silver rouble.   What people often mean by understanding.   Is it possible to understand and disagree?   Are different understandings of the same thing possible?   How people of different levels understand things.   Inner and outer circles of humanity.   Divisions of the inner circle.   The outer circle as the circle where people do not understand one another.   The possibility of understanding depends on penetration into the inner circle.   The language of the inner circle.   Can one see another man's being?   Further study of centres.   Division of each centre into three parts: mechanical, emotional and intellectual.   Study of attention.   Formatory thinking.   Intellectual parts of centres.   What happens when a man begins to remember himself.

I n relation to the study of man's possible development I must establish one very important point.

There are two sides of man that must be developed, i.e. there are two lines of possible development that must proceed simultaneously.

These two sides of man, or two lines of possible development, are *knowledge* and *being*.

I have already spoken many times about the necessity for the development of knowledge, and particularly self-knowledge, because one of the most characteristic features of man's present state is that *he does not know himself.*

Generally people understand the idea of different levels of knowledge, the idea of the relativity of knowledge and the necessity for quite new knowledge.

What people do not understand in most cases is the idea of *being* as quite separate from knowledge; and further, the idea of the relativity of being, the possibility of different levels of being and the necessity for the development of being, separately from the development of knowledge.

66

A Russian philosopher, Vladimir Solovieff, used the term 'being' in his writings. He spoke about the being of a stone, the being of a plant, the being of an animal, the being of a man and the divine being.

This is better than the ordinary concept because in ordinary understanding the being of a man is not regarded as in any way different from the being of a stone, the being of a plant or the being of an animal. From the ordinary point of view a stone, a plant, an animal *are* or *exist* exactly as a man is or exists. In reality they exist quite differently. But Solovieff's division is not sufficient. There is no such thing as *the being of a man*. Men are too different for that. I have already explained that, from the point of view of the system we are studying, the concept of man is divided into seven concepts: man No. 1, man No. 2, man No. 3, man No. 4, man No. 5, man No. 6 and man No. 7. This means seven degrees or categories of being: being No. 1, being No. 2, being No. 3 and so on. In addition to this we already know still finer divisions. We know that there may be very different men No. 1, very different men No. 2 and very different men No. 3. They may live entirely under influences *a*. They may be equally affected by influences *a* and *b*. They may be more under influences *b* than *a*. They may have a magnetic centre. They may have come into contact with school influence or influence *c*. They may be on the way to becoming men No. 4. All these categories indicate different levels of being.

The idea of being entered into the very foundation of thinking and speaking about man in religious thought, and all other divisions of man were regarded as unimportant in comparison with this. Men were divided into sinners, heretics and unbelievers on the one hand, and on the other hand into religious men, good men, righteous men, pious men, saints, martyrs, prophets and so on. All these definitions referred not to differences in views and convictions, i.e. not to knowledge, but to differences in being.

In modern thought people ignore the idea of being and

different levels of being. On the contrary, they believe that the more discrepancies and contradictions there are in a man's being, the more interesting and brilliant he can be. It is generally, although tacitly—and not always even tacitly—admitted that a man can be given to lying, he can be selfish, unreliable, unreasonable, perverted, and yet be a great scientist or a great philosopher or a great artist. Of course this is quite impossible. This incompatibility of different features of one's being, which is generally regarded as originality, actually means weakness. One cannot be a great scholar or a great thinker or a great artist with a perverted or an inconsistent mind, just as one cannot be a prize-fighter or a circus athlete with consumption. The widespread acceptance of the idea that inconsistency and amorality means originality is responsible for the many scientific, artistic and religious fakes of our present time and probably of all times.

It is necessary to understand clearly what *being* means, and why it must grow and develop side by side with knowledge, but independently of it.

If knowledge outgrows being or being outgrows knowledge, the result is always a one-sided development, and a one-sided development cannot go far. It is bound to come to some inner contradiction of a serious nature and stop there.

Some time later we may speak about the different kinds and the different results of one-sided development. Ordinarily in life we meet with only one kind, i.e. where knowledge has outgrown being. The result takes the form of a dogmatization of certain ideas with the consequent impossibility of a further development of knowledge because of the loss of understanding.

Now I shall speak about understanding.

What is understanding?

Try to ask yourself this question, and you will see that you cannot answer it. You have always confused *understanding* with *knowing* or having information. But to know and to understand are two quite different things, and you must learn to distinguish between them.

In order to understand a thing, you must see its connection with some bigger subject, or bigger whole, and the possible consequences of this connection. Understanding is always the understanding of a smaller problem in relation to a bigger problem.

For instance, suppose I show you an old Russian silver rouble. It was a piece of money the size of a half-crown and corresponding to two shillings and a penny. You may look at it, study it, notice in which year it was coined, find out everything about the Tsar whose portrait is on one side, weigh it, even make a chemical analysis and determine the exact quantity of silver contained in it. You can learn what the word 'rouble' means and how it came into use. You can learn all these things and probably many more, but you will not *understand it and its meaning* if you do not find out that before the last war its purchasing power corresponded in many cases to a present-day English pound, and that the present-day paper rouble in Bolshevik Russia corresponds in many cases to an English farthing or even less. If you find out this you will *understand* something about a rouble and perhaps also about some other things, because the understanding of one thing immediately leads to the understanding of many other things.

Often people even think that understanding means finding a name, a word, a title or a label for a new or unexpected phenomenon. This finding or inventing of words for incomprehensible things has nothing to do with understanding. On the contrary, if we could get rid of half of our words perhaps we should have a better chance of a certain understanding.

If we ask ourselves what it means to understand or not to understand a man, we must first think of an instance of not being able to speak with a man in his own language. Naturally two people having no common language will not understand one another. They must have a common language or agree on certain signs or symbols by which they will designate things. But suppose that during a conversation with a man you disagree about the meaning of certain words or signs or symbols, then you again cease to understand each other.

From this follows the principle that you *cannot understand and disagree*. In ordinary conversation we very often say: 'I understand him but I do not agree with him'. From the point of view of the system we are studying, this is impossible. If you understand a man, you agree with him; if you disagree with him, you do not understand him.

It is difficult to accept this idea and this means that it is difficult to understand it.

As I have just said, there are two sides of man which must develop in the gradual course of his evolution: knowledge and being.

Understanding may be compared to an *arithmetical mean* between knowledge and being. It shows the necessity for a simultaneous growth of knowledge and being. The growth of only one of them will not sufficiently increase the growth of the arithmetical mean.

This also explains why to understand means to agree. People who understand one another must not only have an equal knowledge, they must also have an equal being. Only then is mutual understanding possible.

Another wrong idea which people have, or which belongs particularly to our times, is that understanding can be different, that people *can,* i.e. have the right, to understand the same thing differently.

This is quite wrong from the point of view of the system. Understanding cannot be different. There can only be one *understanding;* the rest is non-understanding or incomplete understanding.

But at the same time people do understand things differently. How can we find an explanation of this seeming contradiction?

In reality, there is no contradiction. Understanding means understanding of a part in relation to the whole. But the idea of the whole can be very different in people according to their knowledge and being. This is why the system is again necessary. People learn to understand by understanding the system and everything else in relation to the system.

Complete understanding of everything that a man can understand is the understanding of man No. 7. The understanding of man No. 6 is more theoretical, and the understanding of man No. 5 is more philosophical, although it must be understood that these shades cannot be clearly distinguished by us. The understanding of man No. 4 approaches that of man No. 5, but it is impermanent, i.e. it may be there at one moment and disappear at another moment. Understanding on the level of man No. 1, No. 2 and No. 3 is not understanding at all. Only through the study of the system can one gradually acquire the understanding of man No. 4. After that one may acquire the understanding of man No. 5, and then the understanding of man No. 6.

But speaking on an ordinary level without the idea of a school or a system, one must admit that there are as many understandings as there are people. Everyone understands everything in his own way or according to one or another mechanical training, but this is all a subjective and relative understanding. The way to objective understanding lies through school systems and the change of being.

In order to explain this I must return to the division of man into seven categories.

You must realize that there is a great difference between men No. 1, 2 and 3 and men of higher categories. In reality the difference is much greater than we can imagine. It is so great that all life from this point of view is regarded as being divided into two concentric circles: the inner circle and the outer circle of humanity.

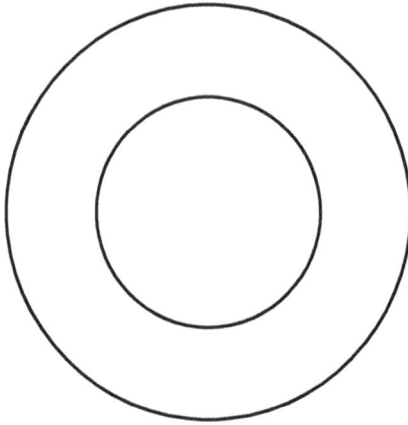

To the inner circle belong men No. 5, 6 and 7; to the outer circle, men No. 1, 2 and 3. Men No. 4 are on the threshold of the inner circle or between the two circles.

The inner circle is, in its turn, divided into three concentric circles; the innermost to which belong men No. 7, the middle to which belong men No. 6 and the outer-inner circle to which belong men No. 5.

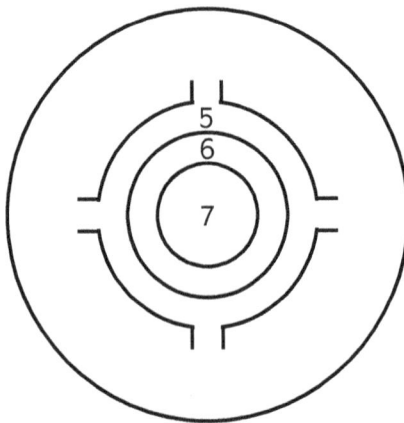

This division does not concern us at the moment. For us, the three inner circles form one inner circle.

The outer circle in which we live has several names, designating its different features. It is called the mechanical circle, because everything *happens* there, everything is mechanical and the people who live there are *machines.* It is also called the *circle of the confusion of tongues,* because people who live in this circle all speak in different languages and *never understand one another.* Everyone understands everything differently.

We have come to a very interesting definition of understanding. It is something that belongs to the inner circle of humanity and does not belong to us at all.

If men in the outer circle realize that they do not understand one another, and if they feel the need of understanding, they must try to penetrate into the inner circle, because understanding between people is possible only there.

Schools of different kinds serve as gates through which people can pass into the inner circles. But this penetration into the circle higher in comparison with the one in which a man is born requires long and difficult work.

The very first step in this work is the study of a new language.

Now you may ask: What is this language we are studying?

And now I am able to answer you.

It is the language of the inner circle, the language in which people can understand one another.

You must realize that standing, so to speak, outside the inner circle we can know only the rudiments of this language. But even these rudiments will help us to understand one another better than we could ever understand without them.

The three inner circles have each a language of their own. We are studying the language of the *outer* of the inner circles. People in the outer-inner circle study the language of the middle circle, and people in the middle circle study the language of the innermost circle.

If you ask me how all this can be proved I will answer that it can be proved only by further study of oneself and further observation. If we find that we can understand ourselves and other people, *or certain books,* or certain ideas, better than we could understand them before, and particularly if we find definite facts which show that this better understanding develops, that will be, if not proof, at least a sign of the possibility of proof.

We must remember that our understanding, exactly as our consciousness, is not always on the same level. It is always moving up and down. That means that at one moment we understand more and at another moment we understand less. If we notice these differences of understanding in ourselves, we shall be able to realize that there is a possibility, first, of keeping to those higher levels of understanding and second, of surpassing them.

But theoretical study is not sufficient. You must work on your being and on the change of your being.

If you formulate your aim from the point of view that you wish to understand other people, you must remember one very important school principle: you can understand other people only as much as you understand yourself and *only on the level of your own being.*

This means that you can judge other people's knowledge, but you cannot judge their being. You can see in them only as much as you have in yourself. But people always make the mistake of thinking that they can judge other people's being. In reality, if they wish to meet and *understand* people of higher development than themselves, they must work with the aim of changing their being.

Now we must return to the study of centres and to the study of attention and self-remembering, because these *are the only ways to understanding.*

Besides the division into two parts, positive and negative which, as we saw, is not the same in different centres, each of the four centres is divided into three parts. These three parts correspond to the definition of centres themselves. The first

74

part is 'mechanical', including moving and instinctive principles, or one of them predominating; the second is 'emotional'
and the third is 'intellectual'. The following diagram shows the
position of parts in the intellectual centre. The centre is divided
into positive and negative parts, and each of these two parts is
divided into three parts. Thus the intellectual centre actually
consists of six parts.

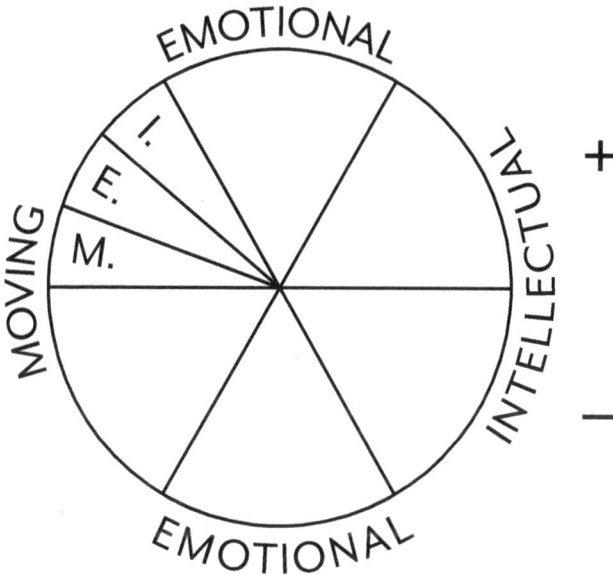

Each of these six parts is in its turn sub-divided into three
parts: mechanical, emotional and intellectual. But about this
sub-division we shall speak much later with the exception of one
part, i.e. the mechanical part of the intellectual centre, about
which I shall speak presently.

The division of a centre into three parts is very simple. A
mechanical part works almost automatically; *it does not require any
attention*. But because of this it cannot adapt itself to a change
of circumstances, it cannot 'think', and it continues to work in
the way it started when circumstances have completely changed.

In the intellectual centre the mechanical part includes in itself all the work of registration of impressions, memories and associations. This is all that it should do normally, i.e. when other parts do their work. It should never *reply* to questions addressed to the whole centre, it should never try to solve problems, and it should never decide anything. Unfortunately, in actual fact, it is always ready to decide, and it always replies to questions of all sorts in a very narrow and limited way, in ready-made phrases, in slang expressions, in party slogans. All these, and many other elements of our usual reactions, are the work of the mechanical part of the intellectual centre.

This part has its own name. It is called a 'formatory apparatus' or sometimes a 'formatory centre'. Many people, particularly people No. 1, i.e. the great majority of mankind, live all their lives with the formatory apparatus only, never touching other parts of their intellectual centre. For all the immediate needs of life, for receiving *a* influences and responding to them, the formatory apparatus is quite sufficient.

It is always possible to recognize 'formatory thinking'. For instance, formatory centre can count only up to two. It always divides everything into two: 'bolshevism and fascism', 'workers and bourgeois', 'proletarians and capitalists' and so on. We owe most modern catchwords to formatory thinking, and not only catchwords but all modern popular theories. Perhaps it is possible to say that at all times all popular theories are formatory.

The emotional part of the intellectual centre consists chiefly of what is called an *intellectual emotion,* i.e. desire to know, desire to understand, satisfaction of knowing, dissatisfaction of not knowing, pleasure of discovery and so on, although again all these can manifest themselves on very different levels.

The work of the emotional part requires full attention, *but in this part of the centre attention does not require any effort.* It is attracted and held by the subject itself, very often through identification, which is usually called 'interest' or 'enthusiasm' or 'passion' or 'devotion'.

The intellectual part of the intellectual centre includes in itself a capacity for creation, construction, invention and discovery. It cannot work without attention, *but the attention in this part of the centre must be controlled* and kept there by will and effort.

This is the chief criterion in studying parts of centres. If we take them from the point of view of *attention* we shall know at once in which part of centres we are. Without attention or with attention wandering, we are in the mechanical part; with the attention attracted by the subject of observation or reflection and kept there, we are in the emotional part; with the attention controlled and held on the subject by will, we are in the intellectual part.

At the same time, the same method shows how to make the intellectual parts of centres work. By observing attention and trying to control it, we compel ourselves to work in the intellectual parts of centres, because the same principle refers to all centres equally, although it may not be so easy for us to distinguish intellectual parts in other centres as, for instance, the intellectual part of the instinctive centre, which works without any attention that we can perceive or control.

Let us take the emotional centre. I will not speak at present about negative emotions. We will take only the division of the centre into three parts: mechanical, emotional and intellectual.

The *mechanical* part consists of the cheapest kind of ready-made humour and a rough sense of the comical, love of excitement, love of spectacular shows, love of pageantry, sentimentality, love of being in a crowd and part of a crowd; attraction to crowd emotions of all kinds and complete disappearance in lower half-animal emotions: cruelty, selfishness, cowardice, envy, jealousy and so on.

The *emotional* part may be very different in different people. It may include in itself a sense of humour or a sense of the comical,

77

as well as religious emotion, aesthetic emotion, moral emotion and, in this case, it may lead to the awakening of *conscience*. But with identification it may be something quite different. It may be very ironical, sarcastic, derisive, cruel, obstinate, wicked and jealous—only in a less primitive way than the mechanical part.

The *intellectual* part of the emotional centre (with the help of the intellectual parts of the moving and the instinctive centres) includes in itself the power of artistic creation. In those cases where the intellectual parts of the moving and the instinctive centres which are necessary for the manifestation of the creative faculty are not sufficiently educated or do not correspond to it in their development, it may manifest itself in dreams. This explains the beautiful and artistic dreams of otherwise quite unartistic people.

The intellectual part of the emotional centre is also the chief seat of the magnetic centre. I mean that if magnetic centre exists only in the intellectual centre it cannot be strong enough to be effective and is always liable to make mistakes or fail. But, when it is fully developed and working with its full power, the intellectual part of the emotional centre is a way to higher centres.

In the moving centre, the mechanical part is automatic. All automatic movements and movements which in ordinary language are called 'instinctive' belong to it, as well as imitation and the capacity for imitation which plays such a big part in life.

The emotional part of the moving centre is connected chiefly with the pleasure of movement. Love of sport and of games should *normally* belong to this part of the moving centre, but when identification and other emotions become mixed with it, it is very rarely there, and in most cases the love of sport is in the moving part of either the intellectual or the emotional centres.

The intellectual part of the moving centre is a very important and a very interesting instrument. Everyone who has ever done *well* any physical work, whatever it may have been, knows that every kind of work needs many *inventions*. One has to invent one's own small methods for everything one does. These inventions are the work of the intellectual part of the moving centre, and many other inventions of man also need the work of the intellectual part of the moving centre.

The power of imitating *at will* the voice, intonations and gestures of other people, *such as actors possess,* also belongs to the intellectual part of the moving centre; but when this power is very highly developed, it is mixed with the work of the intellectual part of the emotional centre.

The work of the instinctive centre is very well hidden from us. We really know, i.e. feel and can observe, only the sensory and emotional part.

The mechanical part includes in itself habitual sensations which very often we do not notice at all, but which serve as a background to other sensations; also *instinctive movements* in the correct meaning of the expression, i.e. all inner movements such as the circulation of the blood, the movement of food in the organism and inner and outer reflexes.

The intellectual part is very big and very important. In the state of self-consciousness or approaching it, one can come into contact with the intellectual part of the instinctive centre and learn a great deal from it concerning the functioning of the machine and its possibilities. The intellectual part of the instinctive centre is the mind behind all the work of the organism, a mind quite different and separate from the intellectual mind.

The study of parts of centres and their special functions requires a certain degree of self-remembering. Without remembering oneself one cannot observe for a sufficiently long time or sufficiently clearly to feel and understand the difference of functions belonging to different parts of different centres.

The study of attention shows the parts of centres better than anything, but the study of attention again requires a certain amount of self-remembering.

Very soon you will realize that all your work upon yourself

is connected with self-remembering and that it cannot proceed successfully without this. And self-remembering is a *partial awakening,* or the beginning of awakening. Naturally—and this must be very clear—*no work can be done in sleep.*

INDEX

imagine

strange Book observing unfortunately circumstances
expression

disappear unpleasant explain name chance big desire speaking
awakening wish unity particularly definition place
developed generally modern form speak belong place naturally
manifestation important play help positive rarely scientific
create strong present reality born learn connected identification special suppose
sufficiently good kinds
necessity relation understanding observe develop physical
organism personality function fact system attention basis
waking moving extent sign development level categories
suffering speed truth action understood
theories impossible parts art mental feature machine
method real change essence moment consciousness question lying science equally awaken
pleasant dream religion circle four taste possesses
realization wrong centre psychology animal
created artificial evolution possible objective bad self-study consist
acquiring dislike possibility man idea realize word rolls
debut ascribe meet clear division live philosophy power and
relative show sleep negative life work useful obstacle
require movement line language period
magnetic term divided school study knowledge effort capacity
self-remembering believe intellectual higher love chief exactly growth
difficulty emotional human side course difference small
qualities struggle feelings impression cases return Lecture degree body
notice mechanical influence ordinary imagination smell
beings psychological conscious remember acquire ask sufficient
normal nature conditions observation order existence acquired
contradiction produce difficult remain
belonging long free permanent self-consciousness particular absence
illusion material principle position
existed useless teaching harmful gravity
self-observation imitation
imaginary

www.ingramcontent.com/pod-product-compliance
Lightning Source LLC
Chambersburg PA
CBHW021821090426
42811CB00028B/1932